WHY THE SHEDDING OF THE BLOOD?

The Effects Of The Blood Of Jesus In Our Lives

MONIKA STAROVA

COPYRIGHT © 2025
Monika Starova

All rights are reserved. No part of this book may be reproduced, distributed, or transmitted in any form or by any means, including photocopying, recording, or other electronic or mechanical methods, without the prior written permission of the author, except in the case of brief quotations embodied in critical reviews and certain other noncommercial uses permitted by copyright law. For permission requests, write to the author at the address provided in the acknowledgments section of this book.

Printed in the United States of America

First Printing Edition, 2025

Dedication

I dedicate this book to my dear father, who passed away and gave his life to Jesus in 2021.

Author's Note

The blood of Jesus Christ is the most precious blood. It refers to His physical blood shed on the cross for the salvation of humanity. Scripture makes this clear: *"knowing that you were not redeemed with corruptible things, like silver or gold, from your aimless conduct received by tradition from your fathers, but with the precious blood of Christ, as of a lamb without blemish and without spot"* (1 Peter 1:18–19, NKJV). And again, *"according to the law almost all things are purified with blood, and without shedding of blood there is no remission"* (Hebrews 9:22, NKJV).

The blood of Jesus redeems us from sin, forgives us, and delivers us from the hand of the devil. It is the heart of the Gospel. His blood speaks for us in heaven and on earth. When Jesus rose from the dead, He carried His blood into heaven and sprinkled it on the heavenly mercy seat as part of His priestly work (John 20:17). Just as the blood of Abel cried out from the ground for justice after Cain killed him (Genesis 4:10–11), the blood of Jesus cries out for mercy and forgiveness (Hebrews 12:24). Abel's blood was shed unwillingly, but Jesus willingly shed His blood to save us.

Through His blood, we are justified, sanctified, and given eternal life. Scripture declares: *"In Him we have redemption through His blood, the forgiveness of sins, according to the riches of His grace"* (Ephesians 1:7, NKJV). And again: *"Let the redeemed of the Lord say so"* (Psalm 107:2). His blood still speaks today with power to redeem, heal, purify, and reconcile us to God.

This is why I testify boldly: the blood of Jesus is alive, powerful, and eternal. It continues to intercede for us before the Father, securing our victory and our salvation.

Preface

This book was born out of a lifelong journey of faith and a deep desire to understand the mystery and power of the blood of Jesus Christ. Since I gave my life to Christ as a child in 1991, I have continually witnessed how His blood has protected, guided, and redeemed me and my family. Through many challenges – spiritual, emotional, and physical – I have come to believe with all my heart that there is no victory, no healing, and no lasting peace apart from the blood of Jesus.

I was born in Albania, and in 1998, I moved to Switzerland to study French at university, where I lived for eight years. In 2006, I immigrated on my own to Canada and have since made my home in Toronto, Ontario. Today, I work as a paralegal, notary, and French teacher at Holy Name of Mary Catholic College. Alongside my professional life, I am an evangelist, called to share the gospel of Jesus Christ throughout the city. Whether in the classroom, on the street, or in daily encounters, my passion is to see people healed, set free, and transformed by the power of the blood of Jesus.

The purpose of this book is to help others discover what I have experienced personally: the living power of Jesus' sacrifice and how to apply it in everyday life. The blood of Jesus is not only for our forgiveness, but for our complete transformation. It speaks on our behalf in the courts of heaven, cleanses us daily, and gives us boldness to approach the throne of grace. It is through His blood that we are redeemed, justified, sanctified, and restored.

Many people believe in the truth of Christ's sacrifice, but few know how to proclaim it with faith. This book explores how the blood of Jesus works when combined with the Word of God and our spoken confession. The Bible says that life and death are in the power of the tongue. When we speak the promises of God with faith and boldness, aligning our words with His truth, we give power to what Christ has already accomplished for us.

I pray that the words in this book help you draw closer to the heart of Jesus, discover the authority you have in Him, and live in the freedom, protection, and eternal life that His blood provides. May it inspire you to speak His truth daily, walk boldly in faith, and enter into the full inheritance that God has prepared for His children.

Monika Starova

Contents

Dedication ii

Author's Note iii

Preface v

Introduction ix

Chapter One: The Significance Of Blood In Ancient Covenants 1

Chapter Two: The History Of Blood Sacrifice 12

Chapter Three: The Blood Of Jesus: From The Old To The New Covenant 26

Chapter Four: The Power Of Blood In Spiritual Warfare 36

Chapter Five: Healing Through The Blood 46

Chapter Six: The Communion: The Power Of The Bread And The Cup .. 55

Chapter Seven: The Power Of Proclamation 65

Chapter Eight: The Effects Of Blood In Daily Life 75

Chapter Nine: Breaking Curses And Strongholds Through Blood 94

Chapter Ten: Ten Effects Of The Blood Of Jesus 106

Chapter Eleven: Jesus: Fully Man And Fully God 121

Chapter Twelve: The Blood And The Church Today 130

Chapter Thirteen: The Legacy Of The Blood: Eternal Life & Beyond..... 140

Chapter Fourteen: Prayers Of Proclamation 145

Conclusion 157

Introduction

Without the blood of Jesus Christ, there is no victory in our lives, and there is no remission of sins. It is because of the blood of Jesus that we have eternal life; death no longer has power over us. The blood of Jesus entitles us to be written in the Lamb's Book of Life (Revelation 13:8).

We live in an evil world, a world that Satan controls. He has reigned here since the fall of Adam and Eve. The world lies in the power of the wicked one – Satan – as we see in Revelation 12. The Devil was cast down to the earth, and his angels were cast out with him. The word "Devil" comes from the Greek word *Diabolos* and the Latin *Diabolo*, meaning "the accuser" or "the adversary." He is the enemy, the one who opposes and resists; he is described as a dragon and a snake. His primary aim is to deceive the whole world.

This is why we need deliverance from the evil in this world and its bondage. We cannot allow the evil in the world to control our thinking. The blood of Jesus redeems us from sin, makes us righteous, justifies us in the heavenly court, gives us life instead of death, heals us, forgives our sins, and enables us to stand before God as kings and queens in Christ.

The blood of Jesus is powerful. Even a single drop shakes heaven, earth, and the powers of hell. There is immense power in the precious, pure, and unblemished blood of Jesus. Through His blood, God offers us not just redemption on earth but eternal life beyond this world. Jesus took all our sins upon Himself – everything from the rebellion of Adam onward – through His sacrifice on the cross.

Jesus' crucifixion brought victory over Satan, and it is through the shedding of His blood that we receive this victory. This is why Jesus had to shed His blood – so that He could become a curse for us and, through His sacrifice, we might receive the blessings of God in all aspects of our lives: in marriage, work, health, finances, and happiness (Galatians 3:13-14). However, these blessings are only activated when we proclaim the blood of Jesus daily in our lives, through the Word of God.

Hebrews 4:14 (NKJV) reminds us: "Seeing then that we have a great High Priest who has passed through the heavens, Jesus the Son of God, let us hold fast our confession." This means that our confession, or proclamation, is crucial in the court of heaven. Our words are what engage heaven, and it is through our proclamation of the blood of Jesus that His work is activated in our lives. It is essential that we speak the right proclamations that make Jesus our mediator before God.

Attitude also plays a significant role in this process. A heart of gratitude in every proclamation and daily life is the key to experiencing miracles and breakthroughs. This must be done with faith and boldness in Jesus Christ. As believers, we are engaged in spiritual warfare. Since we are sons and daughters of Christ, the Devil and his demons will try to discourage us, rob us of our faith, and weaken our strength in God. As Apostle Paul says in Hebrews 10, we must hold fast to our confession and insist on the Word of God, no matter the situation.

The blood of Jesus Christ testifies against Satan, declaring that I have been redeemed from his grasp. I have victory over the world, the flesh, and the devil. Through the blood of Jesus Christ, all my sins are forgiven. The blood of Jesus cleanses me continually from all sin. Through His blood, I am justified and made righteous, as if I have never sinned. Every chain that once controlled me has been broken. I am free through the blood of Jesus, set apart for God's purposes. My body is the temple of the Holy Spirit, redeemed and cleansed by the blood of Jesus. Satan has no power over me, and his plans against me are nullified. I am free, redeemed, and empowered by the blood of Jesus. Hallelujah to the Lamb of God! In Jesus Christ, Amen!

Jesus is our Lord and Savior, both fully man and fully God. He is the last Adam, and He will come again to judge the living and the dead. All believers in Christ will live with Him forever (1 Corinthians 15:23).

Since becoming a Christian in 1991 at the age of 11, I have experienced the power of the blood of Jesus and His sacrifice on the cross. For much of my life, the significance of His blood was a mystery. I wrote this book for both believers and non-believers, intending to help them discover Christ and the power of His blood in our lives. Throughout my life, I have witnessed and experienced the favor and protection of God upon me and my family through the application of His blood.

Applying His blood and proclaiming the communion we take is a vital aspect of living a victorious life on earth. But it is not just the blood of Christ – it is the Word of our testimony, our proclamations of faith and boldness. When we are weak, Jesus makes us strong, filling us with joy, breakthrough, hope, and victory. His blood brings us into the throne of grace before the Father, where He hears our prayers and communicates with us. Through His blood, we receive the gift of salvation and eternal life in heaven, where there is joy, peace, and happiness.

The soul of humanity is precious to God. The Lord desires to empty hell and fill heaven with His people. The sacrifice of Jesus on the cross, His suffering – both emotionally and physically – along with His abandonment by all, gives us the assurance that no suffering we endure in this world can compare to what He experienced.

As fully God and fully man, Jesus understands the human experience. Though He was God, He grew up as a simple man. His earthly father was Joseph, a carpenter, and His mother was Mary. But His heavenly Father was the Almighty God, the Creator of all things. Jesus grew up and worked as a carpenter, as we see in Mark 6:3, but He was also the Son of God and God Himself. The Trinity – the Father, Son, and Holy Spirit – are one (John 14).

Jesus knows our suffering because He endured much during His ministry. He was beaten and tortured by Roman soldiers (John 19:1, Mark 15:15, Matthew 27:26). He was rejected by the people in the synagogue (Luke 4:14-30). He experienced hunger (Mark 11:12) and tiredness (John 4:6), just like we do as human beings. Jesus also felt sadness and sorrow. We see His tears when He learned that Lazarus had died and had been buried for four days (John 11:35). Jesus was also tempted by Satan during the beginning of His ministry. After fasting for 40 days, He was tempted in the desert, but unlike us, He did not submit to temptation. He resisted Satan using the Word of God, as we see in Matthew 4:1-11, where He quotes from Deuteronomy 8:3.

Even in the Garden of Gethsemane, when He faced the temptation to give up on going to the cross (Luke 22:42), Jesus prayed consistently, battling the temptation but remaining victorious. The goodness of Jesus is evident in His obedience to the Father, as we see in Matthew 26:63.

As the Son of God and the Son of Man, Jesus exhibited an immense love for us, a love that surpasses human understanding. His crucifixion was the ultimate act of love, as He chose to set aside His own will and obey His Heavenly Father to sacrifice Himself for us (John 3:16). The love of God in Jesus Christ is so great, it cannot be fully explained in human terms. It is a love without limits, and nothing in this world compares to it.

In order to be a sacrifice for us, Jesus had to take on human flesh. As Hebrews 2:14-17 explains, He became fully human so that He could sacrifice His life for our sins. Jesus, both fully God and fully human, lived a life without sin, in perfect obedience to God the Father.

Through His sinless life and sacrificial death on the cross, Jesus became the Lamb without blemish (1 Peter 1:19). His pure blood paid the price for our sins, and His righteousness is credited to those who place their faith in Him. As 2 Corinthians 5:21 says, "God made Him who had no sin to be sin for us, so that in Him we might become the righteousness of God."

Jesus is the last Adam, and unlike the first Adam, who failed to uphold God's law, Jesus fulfilled it perfectly. Because of His sacrifice, we now have the righteousness of God through His blood. This righteousness is extended to all who have faith in Christ for the forgiveness of their sins (2 Corinthians 5:21).

Jesus' blood is a sacrifice that cleanses us from all sin. Though we are born with a sinful nature, He is willing to forgive us, purify us, and give us eternal life both on earth and in heaven. His love for us is boundless, and He longs for fellowship with us, desiring that we come to know Him more deeply.

After His resurrection, Jesus appeared to His apostles and disciples over the course of 40 days, demonstrating His deity and humanity. He ascended to heaven and is now seated at the right hand of the Father (Mark 16:19, Acts 7:55-56). He is our Lord, our Savior, and our High Priest, interceding for us daily before the Father (Romans 8:34). His communion with the Father is seen in John 17:22, and 1 John 2:1-2 reminds us that Jesus is our advocate, the atoning sacrifice for our sins.

As believers, we are never alone. Jesus has left us the Holy Spirit as our comforter, and the Spirit empowers us to live for Him (John 14:16-26).

Chapter One: The Significance Of Blood In Ancient Covenants

The deity and humanity of Jesus Christ, his crucifixion, his suffering, his victory on the cross, and his resurrection on the third day are mysteries of the Gospels that mankind, with their human logic and mind, cannot, and will never fully understand and perceive.

(Monika Starova)

When Adam and Eve first sinned, their eyes were opened to their nakedness. They knew shame, something they had never experienced before. To cover themselves, they used the skin of an animal, the first instance of blood being shed to cover sin. This act was more than just physical; it was a significant moment. They realized the cost of sin – innocent blood. The animal had to die for their covering, setting the foundation for what would later become the understanding of blood as a means for atonement.

Noah followed this tradition as well. After the flood, Noah built an altar and sacrificed animals to God. It was an act of worship, and through the shedding of blood, Noah communicated with God. This was another sign of the importance of blood in maintaining a connection with the divine, even though the Bible doesn't explicitly mention blood being shed for his covering.

Then came the covenant with Abraham. God tested Abraham's faith, asking him to sacrifice his son Isaac. But just as Abraham was about to follow through, God provided a ram in Isaac's place. Again, blood was shed, and this time, it was a clear signal of a deeper meaning – blood symbolized both protection and promise. This covenant with Abraham showed how blood serves as a sign of faith and obedience, marking the beginning of blessings and protection that only God could grant.

Moses and Aaron took this understanding even further. In their time, the priesthood was established, and the shedding of blood became an official act of covering sin. The Israelites understood that without the blood, there would be no forgiveness. This idea is clear in Leviticus 16:15-19, where the priest had to offer the blood of animals as an atonement for the people's sins. It was a recognition that blood was the only way to cover the sins of the people, and without it, they would face death. Leviticus 17:11 reinforces this: "For the life of the flesh is in the blood, and I have given it to you to make atonement for yourselves on the altar; it is the blood that makes atonement for one's life."

David, too, understood the power of blood. His covenant with God showed that the blood was a necessary component for maintaining the relationship between God and His people. David's sacrifices reflected his dependence on God's grace and protection through the shedding of innocent blood.

But all these covenants and sacrifices pointed towards the ultimate sacrifice – the Messiah. Jesus Christ came to fulfill the prophetic visions of the Old Testament. The shedding of His blood was the final act of atonement, not just for a particular group of people, but for the world. The blood of animals could only cover sin for a time, but Jesus' blood would take it away forever. His sacrifice on the cross marked the end of the old and the beginning of a new covenant – one that was not based on continuous offerings, but on a single, perfect sacrifice.

Jesus' blood did what no other sacrifice could do – it provided redemption, forgiveness, cleansing, and a new birth. His blood has the power to reconcile us with God (Romans 5:10-11). It is by His blood that we are redeemed from eternal separation from God, as stated in Ephesians 1:7, "In Him, we have redemption through His blood, the forgiveness of sins, in accordance with the riches of God's grace."

From Adam and Eve's first sacrifice to the ultimate sacrifice of Jesus, the shedding of blood has always held a deep spiritual significance. It was through blood that sin was covered, and it was through blood that humanity could be reconciled to God. This is why the blood of Jesus is still relevant and powerful today. It was not just a historical event but a continuous source of hope and strength for those who believe. His blood is applicable to our daily lives, reminding us that we are forgiven, redeemed, and covered by the sacrifice He made.

The Old Testament covenant was repeated through various key figures, each playing a significant role in the unfolding plan. God spoke to Abraham and promised blessings, protection, and numerous descendants, but the shedding of blood was central to sealing these promises. The moment Abraham prepared to sacrifice his son, God intervened, providing a ram as a substitute. This act pointed forward, symbolizing Jesus as the ultimate sacrifice. The shedding of blood, starting with the animal, was a pattern that continued, but the people had to follow God's instructions for it to have meaning.

This wasn't just about covering sins temporarily. In the case of Moses, before the Israelites left Egypt, they were commanded to mark their doorposts with the blood of a lamb. Exodus 12:7 recounts, "They are to take some of the blood and put it on the sides and tops of the doorframes of the houses where they eat the lambs." This act protected them from the angel of death, but again, it wasn't the blood alone that did the work. There were actions to be taken – marking the doors, removing yeast from the house, and observing specific ceremonies. The blood had power, but it required their obedience for that power to be realized.

This same principle carries over to the New Testament, where believers are no longer required to offer animal sacrifices, but they must still act in faith. Through the blood of Jesus, a new covenant was formed, one that covers all sins once and for all. But just as in the Old Testament, action is required. Christians partake in communion, which recalls the blood of Christ and serves as a proclamation of His death and resurrection. The act of communion is not just a ritual but a means of applying the significance of His blood to their lives. As the Apostle Paul wrote in 1 Corinthians 11:25, "In the same way, after supper he took the cup, saying, 'This cup is the new covenant in my blood; do this, whenever you drink it, in remembrance of me.'"

Noah, Abraham, Moses, Aaron, and David all followed this pattern of sacrifice and bloodshed. Noah, after being saved from the flood, offered burnt sacrifices, marking the importance of giving thanks through the shedding of blood. David, a man after God's own heart, made sacrifices that not only atoned for sins but also served as a sign of his devotion and dependence on God's mercy.

WHY THE SHEDDING OF THE BLOOD?

The priesthood, established under Aaron, took these principles further. Every year, on the Day of Atonement, the high priest would enter the Holy of Holies with the blood of animals to atone for the sins of the people. Leviticus 16 describes how the priest would sacrifice a goat and sprinkle its blood on the mercy seat to cover the sins of Israel. This was done year after year, but it was always a temporary solution.

The concept of the scapegoat also appears in these rituals. One goat was sacrificed, while the other was sent away, symbolically carrying the sins of the people into the wilderness. Leviticus 16:10 describes this: "But the goat chosen by lot as the scapegoat shall be presented alive before the Lord to be used for making atonement by sending it into the wilderness as a scapegoat." This practice was a clear representation of how sin needed to be removed, but it was incomplete without the blood sacrifice.

All these rituals and sacrifices laid the groundwork for the coming of Jesus. His blood would serve as the final, perfect sacrifice. Hebrews 9:12 explains it clearly: "He did not enter by means of the blood of goats and calves; but he entered the Most Holy Place once for all by his own blood, thus obtaining eternal redemption." The old system required repeated sacrifices, but Jesus' sacrifice was enough to cover all sins, once and for all.

The Old Testament covenants – whether with Noah, Abraham, or Moses – were always pointing to something greater. They were signposts leading to the ultimate covenant, fulfilled in Jesus. His blood doesn't just cover sin temporarily; it removes it entirely. This is why the blood of Jesus is referred to as powerful, not just historically, but in the lives of believers today. It works in ways that the old sacrifices never could, offering eternal redemption and an unbreakable connection with God.

The message of bloodshed that runs throughout the Bible is not just about death; it's about life, protection, and reconciliation. It is the key to understanding the relationship between God and humanity, from the beginning with Adam and Eve, through the covenants with the patriarchs, to the final fulfillment in Christ. His blood continues to provide the same protection, blessing, and covering that was promised long ago.

The Old Testament sacrifices were a clear preparation for the coming of Jesus. Everything that was done – the shedding of blood, the rituals, the altars – pointed to the future fulfillment in Christ. The priests, especially Aaron, played a crucial role in these ceremonies. For instance, as the high priest, Aaron was instructed to sprinkle the blood seven times in the Holy of Holies (Leviticus 16:14): "He is to take some of the bull's blood and with his finger sprinkle it on the front of the atonement cover; then he shall sprinkle some of it with his finger seven times before the atonement cover." This act symbolized purification and atonement, and it prefigured Jesus' ultimate sacrifice. Just as Aaron applied the blood in the holiest place, Jesus applied His blood, not just in a physical temple, but in a spiritual sense, covering humanity's sins for all time.

The connection between the Old Testament and the New Testament is evident. The priestly actions of sprinkling the blood, following God's specific instructions, were a shadow of what was to come. In the New Testament, Jesus shed His blood, not only fulfilling the old rituals but completing them in a way that no animal sacrifice ever could. His blood was spread for all, not just for the people of Israel but for the entire world. This is seen clearly in Hebrews 9:12, where it says, "He did not enter by means of the blood of goats and calves; but he entered the Most Holy Place once for all by his own blood, thus securing eternal redemption."

The sacrificial system in the Old Testament was meticulous. The people had to follow every instruction carefully for the sacrifice to be acceptable. Whether it was sprinkling the blood or burning the fat, every detail mattered. In Leviticus 3:16, we see that the fat of the animal was to be burned as an offering to the Lord because it was considered the best part, and eating it was forbidden. Similarly, in the Day of Atonement rituals, the scapegoat was a symbolic act where the sins of the people were transferred to an animal, which was then sent into the wilderness, as described in Leviticus 16:10. The scapegoat represented the removal of sin, but it wasn't enough on its own. The blood sacrifice had to be made as well.

The people of Israel repeatedly found themselves returning to blood sacrifices because their sins were constant. This was part of the reason why their journey to the Promised Land took 40 years instead of two weeks. Their disobedience and idolatry meant that they had to keep performing these rituals to maintain their connection to God. Moses himself had to constantly intervene on behalf of the people, offering sacrifices and atonement, especially after they created the golden calf and turned away from God (Exodus 32).

One of the most symbolic moments in Moses' leadership came when he placed a bronze snake on a pole during the Israelites' journey through the wilderness. In Numbers 21:8-9, God instructed Moses to make a snake and put it on a pole so that anyone bitten by a venomous snake could look at it and live. This act of looking up at the snake symbolized their need for God's intervention. It later became an analogy for Christ in the New Testament, as Jesus referenced it in John 3:14-15, saying, "Just as Moses lifted up the snake in the wilderness, so the Son of Man must be lifted up, that everyone who believes may have eternal life in him." The bronze snake was another foreshadowing of the salvation that would come through Christ's ultimate sacrifice.

The story of the Old Testament covenants and sacrifices is one of preparation and anticipation. These acts of bloodshed were essential for maintaining the people's connection to God, but they were never enough on their own. The people had to keep offering sacrifices, year after year, to cover their sins. But through all these rituals, God was preparing them for something greater – a permanent solution. That solution was Jesus, whose blood didn't just cover sin but removed it completely. The shedding of blood, from the first animal in Eden to the sacrifices of Moses, Noah, and David, pointed to this ultimate sacrifice. The blood of Jesus didn't just fulfill the old covenant; it created a new one, one that would last forever.

The symbolism of the number seven plays a crucial role throughout both the Old and New Testaments. Aaron, as the high priest, was commanded to sprinkle the blood seven times in the Holy of Holies (Leviticus 16:19). This act symbolized completeness and purification, and it wasn't a random number – seven represents divine perfection. Just as God created the world in seven days, the sprinkling of blood seven times signified the fullness of God's plan for redemption. This practice was a precursor to the ultimate sacrifice of Jesus, who also shed His blood seven times during His crucifixion.

In the New Testament, we see the fulfillment of this symbolism in Jesus' sacrifice. He shed His blood seven times – at Gethsemane (Luke 22:44), when He was scourged (John 19:1), when they placed the crown of thorns on His head (Matthew 27:29), when He was nailed to the cross (Matthew 27:35), and finally when a spear pierced His side (John 19:34). Each instance was a step towards the complete and perfect atonement of sin. It wasn't just an event in history; it was the fulfillment of all the Old Testament sacrifices, done once for all. Hebrews 10:12 makes this clear: "But when this priest had offered for all time one sacrifice for sins, he sat down at the right hand of God."

But while the sacrifice was perfect, the application of that sacrifice continues. Just as the people of Israel had to repeatedly offer sacrifices, we are now called to apply Jesus' sacrifice in our lives. This is not done through physical sacrifices anymore, but through faith, prayer, and communion. Communion becomes a powerful symbol of this application. In 1 Corinthians 11:26, Paul writes, "For whenever you eat this bread and drink this cup, you proclaim the Lord's death until he comes." Each time believers partake in communion, they are not just remembering the sacrifice but applying its power to their lives, just as the Israelites applied the blood of the lamb on their doorposts.

What's important to understand is that while Jesus' sacrifice was once for all, His role as our high priest continues. The imagery in Hebrews 7:25 shows this, stating, "Therefore he is able to save completely those who come to God through him, because he always lives to intercede for them." Jesus is still at work, interceding for us in the courts of heaven. His priesthood, like that of Melchizedek, is eternal. The order of Melchizedek, mentioned in Hebrews 7:17, speaks of a priesthood that is not based on lineage or temporary rituals but on an eternal and unchanging order. Melchizedek was both a king and a priest, and Jesus fulfills this dual role – He reigns as King and serves as Priest.

The priesthood of Jesus is unlike that of Aaron or any other Old Testament priest. While they had to perform rituals and sacrifices repeatedly, Jesus' sacrifice was sufficient for all time. Yet, we are still called to apply His blood through faith. When we proclaim His name, when we speak of His sacrifice, Jesus acts as our advocate in the heavenly courts. This is a continuation of His priestly role, as 1 John 2:1 states, "But if anybody does sin, we have an advocate with the Father – Jesus Christ, the Righteous One." His advocacy is ongoing, and every time we apply His blood in faith, He intercedes on our behalf.

The importance of obedience and faithfulness in the Old Testament sacrifices cannot be overlooked. The priests had to follow God's instructions exactly, or they risked death. Leviticus 10:1-2 recounts the story of Nadab and Abihu, Aaron's sons, who offered unauthorized fire before the Lord and were struck down as a result. This showed the seriousness of approaching God in the correct manner. In contrast, Jesus has taken on this burden for us. He fulfilled the law perfectly, and now, through Him, we are able to approach God with boldness, as Hebrews 4:16 encourages us: "Let us then approach God's throne of grace with confidence, so that we may receive mercy and find grace to help us in our time of need."

While the Old Testament priests had to be ceremonially clean, offering sacrifices for their own sins before they could intercede for the people, Jesus was sinless. He needed no such purification, which is why His sacrifice was not just effective but final. Yet, just as the Israelites had to faithfully observe the rituals of their time, we are called to live in obedience today. This obedience involves applying the blood of Jesus to our lives through prayer, faith, and proclamation. The power of Jesus' blood is not automatic; it requires our participation, just as the Israelites had to act in faith by applying the blood to their doorposts.

As we consider the Old Testament sacrifices, the priesthood, and the covenant, it's clear that everything was leading to the perfect and final sacrifice of Jesus. But while the shedding of His blood on the cross was the fulfillment of the old covenant, it also marked the beginning of a new covenant. This new covenant, established in His blood, is eternal, yet it still requires our response. We are called to live in the reality of His sacrifice, applying it to our lives through faith, obedience, and communion with God.

The process continues, not because the sacrifice of Jesus was incomplete, but because the power of His blood is something we must continually engage with. The Old Testament priests had to perform their rituals perfectly, but now we are under grace. Through Jesus, we have access to the Father, and His blood continues to speak on our behalf in the heavenly courts. It's a reminder that while the work of atonement is finished, the application of that work in our lives is ongoing, as we await the day when Jesus will return and reign forever.

Chapter Two: The History Of Blood Sacrifice

I am convinced that the only way of salvation for humanity was for the son of God, God himself, Jesus Christ, to descend to earth in the form of flesh to liberate the fallen world from the chains of sin and the satanic fate of death.

(Monika Starova)

Blood has been a powerful symbol in ancient religious and cultural rituals, representing life, death, and the bond between the divine and humanity. From the beginning of human history, blood sacrifices have been central to expressing faith and seeking forgiveness, especially in the Judeo-Christian tradition. This chapter explores the origins of blood sacrifices, beginning with Adam, whose first act of atonement set the foundation for understanding the purpose of sacrifice.

After Adam and Eve's disobedience in Eden, they became aware of their nakedness and experienced shame, a new and profound feeling of separation from God. To cover themselves, God provided garments of animal skin (Genesis 3:21), requiring the first shedding of innocent blood to cover sin. This act marks the initial sacrifice that symbolizes atonement and the gravity of sin's consequences. Blood, from that point on, became a medium through which humanity could reconnect with God, symbolizing the cost of disobedience.

Following the expulsion from Eden, blood sacrifices became integral to the covenants God made with humanity, each pointing forward to the ultimate atonement through Jesus. Noah, after the flood, built an altar and offered burnt sacrifices, an expression of worship and thanksgiving, as well as a plea for continued favor. These sacrifices illustrated the recurring theme of blood as a means to purify and sanctify humanity's relationship with God.

With each covenant – from Noah's altar to Abraham's willingness to sacrifice Isaac – the Old Testament practices of sacrifice foreshadowed the future, perfect sacrifice of Jesus. Abraham's test, where God replaced Isaac with a ram, underscored the significance of substitutionary sacrifice, where the life of one stood in for another. This early concept of substitution would later become fully realized in the sacrifice of Christ, who died on behalf of humanity.

As God established Israel as His chosen people, He set apart the tribe of Levi to serve as priests under Aaron. These priests were responsible for conducting the sacrifices necessary for the people's atonement. God provided detailed instructions for sacrifices, which had to be strictly followed to maintain holiness. The book of Leviticus outlines these rituals, where the priests would perform sacrificial rites on behalf of the community, creating a system that upheld the covenant between God and His people.

One key verse that captures this is Leviticus 17:11: "For the life of the flesh is in the blood, and I have given it to you to make atonement for yourselves on the altar; it is the blood that makes atonement for one's life." This verse underlines the concept that life resides in blood, making it sacred and an essential means of atonement.

The Tabernacle, a portable sanctuary for worship, was central to the Israelite community and represented the dwelling place of God among His people. Within the Tabernacle was the Holy of Holies, a place so sacred that only the high priest could enter, and only on the Day of Atonement. During this ceremony, the high priest would enter with the blood of a sacrificial animal and sprinkle it on the mercy seat, signifying the forgiveness of sins for the people of Israel.

Leviticus 16:14 provides detailed instructions: "He shall take some of the blood of the bull and sprinkle it with his finger on the mercy seat on the east side; and before the mercy seat, he shall sprinkle some of the blood with his finger seven times." This act of sprinkling blood in the Holy of Holies marked an atonement ritual that temporarily cleansed the people's sins. The symbolic sprinkling of blood seven times emphasized completeness and divine perfection, foreshadowing the ultimate completeness that would come through Christ's sacrifice.

The Day of Atonement (Yom Kippur) was the most sacred day in the Jewish calendar, dedicated to purging the sins of the people. This ritual involved two goats, each serving a symbolic purpose. The first goat was sacrificed as a sin offering, and its blood was brought into the Holy of Holies by the high priest to atone for the sins of Israel. The second goat, known as the scapegoat, bore the sins of the people symbolically and was sent away into the wilderness, carrying those sins with it.

The high priest would lay his hands on the scapegoat, transferring the iniquities of the people onto it, and the goat would be led away, representing the removal of sin from the community. This practice was a powerful foreshadowing of Jesus, who would later be both the sacrificial lamb and the one who would remove sin permanently, not just cover it. The dual nature of the sacrifice – the blood shed for atonement and the scapegoat bearing away sin – captures the essence of Jesus' role as the ultimate sacrifice.

At the moment of Jesus' crucifixion, the veil in the temple – separating the Holy of Holies from the rest of the temple – was torn from top to bottom (Matthew 27:51). This act symbolized a monumental shift: the end of the old covenant and the beginning of the new. The torn veil represented direct access to God, made possible through Jesus' sacrificial death. No longer was an intermediary priest required; through the blood of Christ, believers could now approach God directly.

This transition from Old Testament rituals to the New Testament covenant with Jesus underscored that His sacrifice was sufficient to cleanse sins once and for all. In Hebrews 10:19-20, it says, "Therefore, brothers and sisters, since we have confidence to enter the Most Holy Place by the blood of Jesus, by a new and living way opened for us through the curtain, that is, his body." This passage reveals that Jesus' body became the new curtain, providing believers with unrestricted access to God's presence.

The Old Testament sacrifices had to be repeated annually because they could not permanently remove sin. However, Jesus' sacrifice was unique; it was a perfect, once-for-all atonement for humanity. Hebrews 9:12 explains this, stating, "He did not enter by means of the blood of goats and calves; but he entered the Most Holy Place once for all by his own blood, thus obtaining eternal redemption." Jesus' blood completed and fulfilled the need for any further sacrifices, offering humanity a way to be fully reconciled with God.

The blood of Jesus is not only a historical event but a continuous source of spiritual power and cleansing. For Christians, it represents forgiveness, protection, and the promise of eternal life. By faith, believers today are able to "apply" the blood of Jesus in their lives, remembering His sacrifice and acknowledging the grace and redemption it offers. Ephesians 1:7 emphasizes this: "In Him, we have redemption through His blood, the forgiveness of sins, in accordance with the riches of God's grace." The sacrificial blood of Christ remains effective for believers, providing an unending connection with God through faith.

Blood sacrifices continued as an essential part of ancient worship, representing the cost of sin and the pathway to redemption. The recurring sacrifices throughout Old Testament history each carried a weight that pointed beyond the act itself, foreshadowing the ultimate purpose of sacrifice – complete reconciliation between humanity and God.

When the tabernacle was established in the wilderness, it became the center of Israel's worship. The tent of meeting, particularly the Holy of Holies, served as a sacred space where God's presence dwelt among His people. Only the high priest could enter this innermost place, and only on the Day of Atonement, symbolizing the great cost of approaching God without the covering of blood. The blood sacrifices offered there were a solemn reminder that sin carried a serious consequence: separation from God, which could only be bridged through atonement.

WHY THE SHEDDING OF THE BLOOD?

On this holy day, the priest performed meticulous rituals, each action carrying deep significance. The high priest would first make a sin offering for himself and then enter the Holy of Holies with the blood of a bull or a goat, sprinkling it on the mercy seat. This ritual represented the covering of sins for both the priest and the people, securing the nation's purity before God for another year. The act was repeated annually, emphasizing the limitations of animal sacrifices – they could cover sin but not remove it entirely.

One of the most profound elements of the Day of Atonement involved the use of two goats. The first goat was killed, and its blood was brought into the Holy of Holies to atone for the sins of Israel. The second goat, the scapegoat, was set apart to bear the sins of the people symbolically. The high priest would lay his hands on its head, transferring the iniquities of the entire community onto the animal. This goat was then led away into the wilderness, illustrating the complete removal of sin from the camp.

This practice, with one goat sacrificed and another sent away, reflected the twofold purpose of atonement: the blood offered for cleansing and the scapegoat as a symbol of forgiveness. Sin, symbolically placed on the scapegoat, was carried far from the people, showing that it was both covered by blood and removed from their presence. These actions prefigured the work of Christ, who would offer not only a covering but a complete removal of sin, becoming both the sacrificial offering and the one who "takes away the sins of the world."

Through these ancient rituals, Israel was reminded annually of the gravity of sin and the importance of God's grace in covering their transgressions. Yet, as much as these rituals served their purpose, they were only temporary measures until a perfect sacrifice could be offered.

As the prophets foretold, this ultimate sacrifice would come through the promised Messiah, who would bear the sins of the people once and for all, providing an everlasting solution to the problem of sin.

When Jesus came, He fulfilled every aspect of these sacrifices. His blood was poured out for the forgiveness of sins, accomplishing what the blood of animals never could. The shedding of His blood satisfied the requirement for justice, but it also went beyond justice, offering mercy and reconciliation. Unlike the high priest, who had to reenter the Holy of Holies year after year, Jesus entered the heavenly sanctuary once and remains there as an intercessor for believers. His sacrifice opened the way for all to have direct access to God, a reality symbolized when the veil of the temple was torn from top to bottom at the moment of His death.

The tearing of this veil signified a seismic shift – the end of the old sacrificial system and the beginning of a new covenant. In this new covenant, Jesus Himself becomes the mediator, and His blood the means by which sins are forgiven. No longer would animal sacrifices be needed, as Jesus' blood provided a complete, once-for-all atonement. His death and resurrection marked the fulfillment of every Old Testament sacrifice, culminating in a sacrifice that was both final and eternal.

For early Christians, the blood of Jesus held profound meaning, symbolizing not only the forgiveness of sins but also a new way of life. His blood was seen as a protective covering and a source of power, much like the blood of the Passover lamb that shielded Israel from death. As Paul wrote in Ephesians, "In Him, we have redemption through His blood, the forgiveness of sins, in accordance with the riches of God's grace." This redemption was no longer a temporary covering but a lasting reconciliation, bringing believers into a renewed relationship with God.

Jesus' blood continues to hold a special place in the life of believers today. Through faith, Christians can "apply" His blood to their lives, invoking its power for protection, healing, and forgiveness. Just as the Israelites marked their doorposts with the blood of the Passover lamb, believers can rely on the covering of Jesus' blood for spiritual security. The practice of communion commemorates this sacrifice, reminding Christians of the new covenant each time they drink the cup, symbolizing His blood shed for them.

The connection between blood and covenant is deeply rooted in the ancient world, where blood was the most sacred symbol of life. In the New Testament, the shedding of Jesus' blood formed a bond that was more than ceremonial; it was a transformative act that changed the relationship between God and humanity forever. By His blood, believers are not only forgiven but also justified, sanctified, and ultimately glorified. This process reflects the journey from the old covenant to the new, where God's promises are fulfilled through Christ.

In Hebrews, one can see that "without the shedding of blood, there is no forgiveness." This principle, seen throughout the Old Testament, was completed in the New, with Jesus as the final sacrifice. His blood, unlike that of bulls and goats, does not simply cover sin temporarily but cleanses the conscience, allowing believers to approach God with confidence. The role of blood in atonement, which began with Adam and carried through Noah, Abraham, and Moses, reaches its pinnacle in Jesus, whose blood is uniquely able to purify and redeem eternally.

The symbolism of hyssop, which was used in Old Testament ceremonies, adds further meaning to the application of blood. Hyssop was used to sprinkle blood during purification rituals, symbolizing cleansing. In the New Testament, John's gospel records that when Jesus was on the cross, He was offered a drink on a hyssop branch, connecting His sacrifice with the ancient practice of purification. This act symbolized that His blood would cleanse believers in a way that the Old Testament sacrifices had only hinted at.

For Christians today, the blood of Jesus is more than a historical event; it's a continuous source of grace, power, and renewal. Applying His blood means living in the reality of His sacrifice, invoking its protection and embracing the freedom it provides. The idea of "pleading the blood" over situations is a way for believers to remember and declare the power of Jesus' sacrifice in their lives, recognizing that His blood has authority over sin, sickness, and spiritual opposition.

Many believers also share personal testimonies of how the blood of Jesus has impacted their lives, citing experiences of physical healing, protection, and spiritual breakthrough. These stories serve as reminders that the power of His blood is active and relevant, working in ways that go beyond human understanding. The sacrifice of Jesus is as potent today as it was two thousand years ago, and through faith, believers can continually draw strength and hope from His atonement.

Some have even reported visions or dreams that reinforce the reality of Jesus' sacrifice. In one account, a believer dreamed of witnessing the crucifixion and was struck by the profound love demonstrated by Christ's suffering. Such personal revelations, while subjective, can deepen an individual's appreciation for the sacrifice of Jesus, drawing them into a closer relationship with God. These experiences underscore the timeless relevance of His blood, which transcends historical rituals to provide an enduring foundation for faith.

As the covenant sealed by Jesus' blood continues to shape the lives of believers, it becomes clear that His sacrifice is not confined to the past. Instead, it reaches into the present, offering forgiveness, redemption, and new life to all who accept it. The blood of Jesus remains a vital part of the Christian journey, symbolizing the unbreakable bond between God and humanity and empowering believers to live with purpose, courage, and conviction.

In the Christian life, applying the blood of Jesus represents not just belief but an active faith that invokes His power and protection. This understanding is rooted in the Passover, where the Israelites applied lamb's blood to their doorposts to protect their households from the angel of death. In the same way, believers today "apply" the blood of Jesus in their prayers and declarations, seeking His covering over their lives, families, and situations.

The act of applying Jesus' blood spiritually means declaring His sacrifice over one's life, trusting in its power for forgiveness, healing, and protection. This practice, often referred to as "pleading the blood," is a way to bring the reality of Jesus' sacrifice into daily life, acknowledging that His death and resurrection are still active forces in the believer's journey. Many Christians recount how praying over specific areas of their life with the blood of Jesus has brought transformation, healing, and even deliverance from difficult circumstances.

The book of Revelation offers a powerful image of the overcoming power of Jesus' blood. Revelation 12:11 states, "They triumphed over him by the blood of the Lamb and by the word of their testimony." This verse emphasizes the combination of Jesus' sacrifice and the believer's personal testimony as tools for victory. The blood of Jesus provides the foundation, while the spoken word of faith – the testimony – activates its power in a tangible way.

The role of testimony is significant in Christian life, as it connects individual experiences to the universal power of Jesus' blood. Testimonies of healing, forgiveness, and miraculous intervention serve as reminders that God's work did not end at the cross but continues in the lives of believers. This ongoing connection between Jesus' sacrifice and personal experience strengthens the community of faith, building confidence that His blood still works in the world today.

The blood of Jesus is also tied to spiritual authority. When believers recognize the power of His blood, they understand their position in Christ, redeemed, justified, and empowered. This awareness allows Christians to resist spiritual opposition with confidence, knowing they are covered by His blood. Through prayer and faith, the believer stands in the authority granted by Jesus' sacrifice, declaring freedom from sin and spiritual bondage.

For early Christians, the image of Jesus as both high priest and sacrificial lamb created a profound sense of hope. In His role as high priest, Jesus intercedes for believers, continually presenting His blood before God as a testament of their forgiveness and righteousness. Hebrews 7:25 explains, "Therefore he is able to save completely those who come to God through him, because he always lives to intercede for them." Jesus' ongoing intercession reassures believers that they are never alone; His blood and His prayers are constant sources of support.

The significance of Jesus' blood as a new covenant is deeply symbolic. Unlike the Old Testament sacrifices, which required repeated offerings, His sacrifice is final, establishing a new relationship between God and humanity. Under this new covenant, believers are not bound by the law's requirements for atonement but live in the freedom of grace, justified by faith in Jesus. This shift is marked by the sacrament of communion, a practice that commemorates His sacrifice and reminds believers of the covenant they share with God.

Each time Christians participate in communion, they reflect on Jesus' words: "This cup is the new covenant in my blood; do this, whenever you drink it, in remembrance of me." In taking the cup, believers reaffirm their commitment to live under the covering of His blood, remembering the price He paid and embracing the new life He offers. Communion serves as a tangible act that reconnects believers to the sacrifice of Jesus, allowing them to live out the reality of the new covenant.

Throughout the Bible, the significance of blood is consistently linked to life, purity, and relationship with God. The blood of Jesus encapsulates these themes, serving as the ultimate means of purification and the foundation of the believer's relationship with God. In moments of doubt, fear, or temptation, Christians can recall the power of His blood, knowing it offers both redemption and the strength to overcome.

In prayer, believers often invoke the blood of Jesus as a declaration of faith, covering areas of their life with His protection and committing themselves to His will. This application of Jesus' blood is not a ritual but a recognition of the spiritual authority given to them through His sacrifice. It is a reminder that they are no longer under the weight of sin but free to live in the light of His grace.

Many believers describe spiritual experiences that reinforce their understanding of Jesus' blood. Some have dreams or visions of the crucifixion, where they encounter a vivid reminder of the love and suffering that Christ endured. These experiences often deepen their faith, reminding them of the personal nature of Jesus' sacrifice and the ongoing impact it has on their lives. For these individuals, the blood of Jesus becomes more than doctrine; it becomes a lived reality that influences their actions, thoughts, and relationship with God.

Jesus' crucifixion also fulfills the prophetic imagery of blood sacrifices throughout the Old Testament. The prophets, especially Isaiah, spoke of a suffering servant who would bear the sins of many. In Isaiah 53:5, it is written, "But he was pierced for our transgressions, he was crushed for our iniquities; the punishment that brought us peace was on him, and by his wounds we are healed." This prophecy finds its fulfillment in Jesus, who bore the physical and spiritual wounds necessary for humanity's healing.

In His sevenfold shedding of blood – from Gethsemane to the cross – Jesus fully embodied the sacrificial system of the Old Testament, yet transformed it into something eternally complete. His sacrifice is not only a testament to God's love but a victory over sin, death, and separation from God. For believers, this is a foundation of hope, one that assures them of their place in God's family and their eternal inheritance.

The application of Jesus' blood in Christian life transcends ancient rituals and enters into a dynamic, personal relationship with God. It calls believers to live with faith, to speak boldly of His sacrifice, and to apply His power in their daily struggles and victories. The blood of Jesus is not merely a historical event; it is a living reality that shapes the way Christians engage with the world, anchoring them in a love that is sacrificial, redemptive, and transformative.

As the chapter closes, the full scope of blood's significance in the Bible becomes clear. From Adam's covering to the elaborate sacrificial system, and ultimately to the final sacrifice of Jesus, blood represents the price of redemption and the pathway to reconciliation with God. The story of blood sacrifice is ultimately a story of love – a love that paid the ultimate price to restore humanity to its Creator. Through Jesus' blood, believers find forgiveness, identity, and purpose, empowered to live in freedom and to share the message of redemption with the world.

Chapter Three:
The Blood Of Jesus: From The Old To The New Covenant

The Blood of Jesus Christ has the same power for all mankind. Jesus Christ does not differentiate between human beings. The Lord Jesus Christ loves us unconditionally, and he does not discriminate in his love for all humanity. No human's love can be compared to the love that Christ has for us. He has an amazing love which is unexplainable with our own worldly thinking or imagination.

(Monika Starova)

The crucifixion of Jesus Christ marked a turning point in the spiritual history of humanity, bringing an end to the Old Testament system of animal sacrifices and establishing a New Covenant. This chapter explores the theological significance of Jesus' sacrifice, the prophetic fulfillment of the Old Covenant, and the eternal impact of His shed blood on humanity.

From the earliest days of human history, the concept of blood and covenant has played a central role in humanity's relationship with God. The term "covenant" in Hebrew is *berith*, meaning a binding agreement, and in Greek, it is *diatheke*, which refers to a testament or will. Covenants were sealed with blood as a sign of their permanence and sanctity, symbolizing the life given to uphold the agreement. Jesus' death fulfilled this tradition, as His blood became the seal of the ultimate covenant between God and humanity.

In the Old Testament, the system of animal sacrifices was a temporary solution for humanity's sin, foreshadowing a greater and eternal atonement. These sacrifices took place in the Holy Temple, particularly within the Tabernacle's Holy of Holies. The high priest, representing the people, would enter this sacred space once a year on the Day of Atonement (Yom Kippur). Carrying the blood of sacrificial animals, he would sprinkle it on the mercy seat, symbolizing the covering of sins.

Leviticus 16:14 explains the significance of these rituals: "He shall take some of the blood of the bull and sprinkle it with his finger on the mercy seat on the east side; and before the mercy seat, he shall sprinkle some of the blood with his finger seven times." Despite their sacredness, these sacrifices were incomplete. They could cover sins temporarily, but they could not remove them permanently. Hebrews 10:4 confirms this limitation: "It is impossible for the blood of bulls and goats to take away sins."

The Old Covenant was always meant to point toward the coming Messiah. Jesus' sacrifice fulfilled every aspect of this prophetic system. As Dr. David Jeremiah explains, Jesus, as the federal head of the spiritual race, contrasts with Adam, the federal head of the natural race. While Adam brought sin and death into the world, Jesus brought redemption and eternal life through His sacrifice (Romans 5:12-19). His crucifixion replaced the repetitive cycle of animal sacrifices, providing a single, perfect offering that cleanses sins eternally.

Jesus' dual nature – fully God and fully human – made His sacrifice both unique and final. As a human, He bore the sins of humanity, and as God, His sacrifice held infinite value, capable of redeeming all of creation. This duality is emphasized in John 1:14: "The Word became flesh and made His dwelling among us." By taking on human form, Jesus not only fulfilled the requirements of the Old Covenant but also became the mediator of the New Covenant.

The shedding of His blood was essential because, as Leviticus 17:11 declares, "the life of the flesh is in the blood." Through His death, Jesus offered His life as a ransom for many, achieving what no other sacrifice could. Hebrews 9:12 states, "He did not enter by means of the blood of goats and calves; but He entered the Most Holy Place once for all by His own blood, thus obtaining eternal redemption."

The sacrificial system and prophetic writings of the Old Testament found their fulfillment in Jesus. Passages like Isaiah 53:5 foreshadowed His role as the suffering servant: "But He was pierced for our transgressions, He was crushed for our iniquities; the punishment that brought us peace was on Him, and by His wounds, we are healed." Each detail of His crucifixion aligned with these prophecies, demonstrating that He was the long-awaited Lamb of God.

The Passover lamb in Exodus 12:20-29, whose blood protected the Israelites from the destroyer, prefigured Jesus as the ultimate Passover lamb. John the Baptist proclaimed this truth in John 1:29: "Behold, the Lamb of God who takes away the sin of the world." The blood of the lamb on the doorposts in Egypt symbolized the coming atonement through Christ, whose sacrifice not only protects but also delivers believers from the bondage of sin.

At the moment of Jesus' death, the veil in the temple was torn from top to bottom (Matthew 27:51). This event symbolized the end of the Old Covenant and the beginning of the New. The torn veil granted direct access to God, no longer requiring an intermediary priest. Hebrews 10:19-20 reflects this transition: "Therefore, brothers and sisters, since we have confidence to enter the Most Holy Place by the blood of Jesus, by a new and living way opened for us through the curtain, that is, His body."

The New Covenant established by Jesus' blood is eternal and unbreakable, offering forgiveness and reconciliation to all who believe. His sacrifice replaced the shadows of the Old Testament with the substance of true redemption, fulfilling God's promises and inviting humanity into a renewed relationship with Him.

Jesus' sacrifice on the cross not only fulfilled the requirements of the Old Covenant but also introduced a transformative relationship between God and humanity. This act of atonement, unparalleled in its scope and significance, bridged the gap that sin had created. Through His blood, Jesus brought a new level of spiritual freedom and access to God, marking the completion of centuries of prophecy and divine promises.

The shedding of Jesus' blood carried a depth of meaning that surpassed the rituals of the Old Covenant. While the sacrifices of animals served as temporary measures, Jesus' sacrifice was eternal, offering a permanent resolution to the problem of sin. His dual nature as fully God and fully human ensured that His sacrifice was sufficient for all of humanity while remaining uniquely divine. Unlike the repeated offerings made by the high priests of Israel, Jesus entered the heavenly Holy of Holies once, bringing with Him the power to cleanse humanity from all unrighteousness.

The idea of covenant, as understood in Scripture, reflects a profound commitment between God and His people. In Hebrew, the word *berith* conveys a solemn agreement often ratified with blood, symbolizing life and permanence. In Greek, *diatheke* carries the meaning of a testament or will, emphasizing the fulfillment of divine promises. The blood of Jesus ratified the ultimate covenant, making obsolete the earlier agreements that required continual sacrifices. His blood, offered willingly, became the foundation of a relationship that transcends legalistic requirements, centering instead on grace and redemption.

The transition from the Old Covenant to the New is exemplified in the tearing of the temple veil at the moment of Jesus' death. This physical act carried immense spiritual significance, demonstrating that the separation between humanity and God had been removed. No longer confined to a chosen priesthood, access to God became a universal gift available to all who believed. The temple rituals, once the only means of atonement, gave way to a new reality where forgiveness and restoration were available through faith in Jesus.

Dr. David Jeremiah, in his biblical studies, explains the profound implications of this transition. He contrasts the natural man, represented by Adam, with the spiritual man, embodied by Christ. Adam, as the federal head of the human race, brought sin and death into the world, whereas Jesus, as the head of the redeemed, offered spiritual life and eternal hope. This shift redefined the human condition, moving from condemnation under sin to freedom in Christ. Through His sacrifice, Jesus not only reversed the curse of sin but also secured victory over death itself.

The blood of Jesus is more than a theological concept; it is a living reality with profound implications for believers today. Just as the Israelites applied the blood of the Passover lamb to their doorposts, marking their homes as protected from judgment, Christians are called to apply the blood of Jesus to their lives. This spiritual act signifies trust in His sacrifice and a declaration of His power over sin, death, and the forces of darkness. The application of Jesus' blood is both a reminder of His victory and a source of strength in the face of life's challenges.

In Revelation 12:11, Scripture declares, "They triumphed over him by the blood of the Lamb and by the word of their testimony." This verse emphasizes the dual power of Jesus' blood and the believer's testimony in overcoming spiritual opposition. The blood of Jesus provides the foundation for victory, while the spoken declaration of faith activates its power in daily life. This truth underscores the ongoing relevance of Jesus' sacrifice, which continues to empower believers in their journey of faith.

The universal nature of Jesus' sacrifice is a testament to His boundless love for humanity.

The prophetic promises of the Old Testament find their culmination in Jesus. From the imagery of the Passover lamb to the suffering servant in Isaiah, each element pointed to the Messiah, who would accomplish what no earthly sacrifice could. The blood of Jesus, once shed, fulfilled these promises in their entirety, bringing to completion the divine plan of redemption. His sacrifice was not only an end but also a beginning, establishing a covenant that remains active and effective for all time.

The power of Jesus' blood is not limited to the forgiveness of sins; it also transforms the believer's identity and purpose. Through His blood, Christians are justified, sanctified, and ultimately glorified, becoming new creations in Christ. This transformation is both immediate and ongoing, as the blood of Jesus continues to cleanse and renew those who place their faith in Him. The believer's life becomes a reflection of His sacrifice, marked by love, righteousness, and a commitment to spreading the message of salvation.

The advocacy of Jesus in the heavenly realm is another critical aspect of His role as the mediator of the New Covenant. As Hebrews 7:25 explains, "Therefore He is able to save completely those who come to God through Him, because He always lives to intercede for them." Jesus' blood serves as a continual testimony before God, defending believers against accusations and securing their standing in grace. This ongoing intercession demonstrates that His sacrifice was not merely a historical event but an eternal provision for humanity.

In understanding the significance of Jesus' blood, it becomes clear that His sacrifice was the ultimate fulfillment of every covenant, promise, and prophecy in Scripture. The New Covenant, sealed with His blood, offers a relationship with God that is both personal and profound. Through faith in Jesus, believers are not only reconciled to God but also empowered to live lives that reflect His love and grace. The impact of His blood is felt not only in the spiritual realm but also in the daily lives of those who trust in Him.

The blood of Jesus stands as the defining element of the New Covenant, carrying immense theological and practical implications for believers. While the Old Covenant relied on repeated sacrifices to maintain temporary atonement, Jesus' blood accomplished a permanent and universal redemption. This sacrifice is not only a conclusion to the Old Testament sacrificial system but also the beginning of a transformative relationship between humanity and God.

The concept of applying the blood of Jesus in the lives of believers is rooted in the Passover account in Exodus. Just as the Israelites applied the lamb's blood to their doorframes for protection, Christians spiritually apply the blood of Jesus as a declaration of faith and trust in His sacrifice. This act signifies covering, cleansing, and empowerment, serving as a constant reminder of the victory that Christ's blood has achieved. It reinforces the idea that His sacrifice was not only a historical event but also a continuing source of spiritual power.

Dr. David Jeremiah highlights the distinction between the natural man and the spiritual man in the context of Jesus' redemptive work. Adam's legacy brought sin, death, and separation from God, while Jesus, as the federal head of the spiritual race, brought eternal life and reconciliation. This contrast underscores the transformative power of the New Covenant, which shifts believers from living under the curse of sin to walking in the freedom of grace. Jesus' resurrection, as Jeremiah explains, secures this victory over death, ensuring that believers have eternal life and a future free from the sting of sin.

The advocacy of Jesus in the court of heaven is another profound element of His sacrifice. Hebrews 9:24 reveals that Jesus entered heaven itself to appear for us in God's presence, using His blood as a defense against accusations from the enemy. This imagery emphasizes His role as both the sacrifice and the high priest, continually interceding on behalf of believers. In Revelation 12:10, Satan is described as "the accuser of our brethren," yet Jesus' blood silences these accusations, securing the believer's position in righteousness.

The prophetic imagery of the Passover lamb, the sprinkling of blood on the mercy seat, and the sacrificial rituals of the Old Testament all pointed to the ultimate sacrifice of Christ. His blood fulfilled these prophetic promises, bridging the gap between humanity and God. The tearing of the temple veil at the moment of His death symbolized the removal of barriers, granting believers direct access to God. Through His blood, Christians no longer require an earthly mediator, as Jesus Himself serves as the eternal high priest and advocate.

The blood of Jesus also represents the foundation of the believer's spiritual identity. As 1 Peter 1:18-19 declares, "You were redeemed from the empty way of life handed down to you from your ancestors, not with perishable things such as silver or gold, but with the precious blood of Christ, a lamb without blemish or defect." This redemption transforms believers, calling them to live lives that reflect their newfound freedom and relationship with God. The application of Jesus' blood is not just about forgiveness but also about empowerment to live in the light of His grace.

The victory over sin and death accomplished through Jesus' blood is both final and ongoing. Paul captures this in 1 Corinthians 15:55-57: "Where, O death, is your victory? Where, O death, is your sting? The sting of death is sin, and the power of sin is the law. But thanks be to God! He gives us the victory through our Lord Jesus Christ." This victory is not limited to the spiritual realm but extends to every area of the believer's life, providing strength, hope, and assurance in the face of challenges.

The New Covenant established by Jesus' blood is characterized by its inclusivity and permanence. Unlike the temporary coverings of the Old Covenant, His blood removes sin entirely, reconciling believers to God once and for all. This reconciliation is not merely a restoration of the past but the establishment of a new relationship that transcends human limitations. Through Jesus, believers are adopted into God's family, becoming heirs to His promises and participants in His eternal kingdom.

The practical implications of Jesus' blood are evident in the lives of believers. It provides a source of spiritual authority, enabling Christians to overcome temptation, fear, and spiritual opposition. The act of "pleading the blood" is a declaration of faith, invoking the power of Jesus' sacrifice in prayer and spiritual warfare. It is a reminder that His blood has already secured victory over every challenge, giving believers the confidence to face life's trials with courage and hope.

Jesus' sacrifice also calls believers to live in alignment with His example. The blood of Jesus not only cleanses but also sanctifies, setting believers apart for God's purposes. This sanctification is an ongoing process, as the Holy Spirit works within believers to transform their hearts and minds, conforming them to the image of Christ. Through His blood, Christians are empowered to live lives of integrity, love, and service, reflecting the character of their Savior.

As the chapter concludes, the magnitude of Jesus' sacrifice becomes clear. His blood accomplished what no other sacrifice could, providing eternal redemption and establishing a covenant that cannot be broken. It fulfilled every prophetic promise, bridging the gap between the Old and New Covenants and offering a path of reconciliation for all humanity. The blood of Jesus is not only a theological cornerstone but also a living reality that continues to shape the lives of believers, calling them to walk in the light of His love and grace.

Chapter Four:
The Power Of Blood In Spiritual Warfare

We do not need to be pitiful, or angry or bitter against each other because of the injustices happening to us in this evil worldly life. We need to remember that Christ lives in us and for us forever. That he took all our suffering and bitterness on the cross. That our suffering today is only temporary and cannot be compared to all the suffering, rejection, humiliation, loneliness, and pain he endured because of his love for us.

(Monika Starova)

Spiritual warfare is an integral aspect of the Christian journey, a battle waged not against flesh and blood but against the unseen forces of darkness. The blood of Jesus Christ stands as a powerful weapon in this fight, offering protection, victory, and deliverance for believers. Through His sacrifice, Jesus provided not only salvation but also the means to overcome spiritual attacks, break curses, and dismantle strongholds.

WHY THE SHEDDING OF THE BLOOD?

The spiritual realm is a dynamic and active reality where forces of light and darkness contend. Ephesians 6:12 reminds us, "For we do not wrestle against flesh and blood, but against principalities, against powers, against the rulers of the darkness of this age, against spiritual hosts of wickedness in the heavenly places." Within this realm, the blood of Jesus serves as a divine shield, its application through prayer and proclamation activating its power in the lives of believers.

The blood of Jesus carries the authority to break demonic attacks and spiritual bondage. As 2 Corinthians 10:3-5 explains, "For though we walk in the flesh, we do not war according to the flesh. For the weapons of our warfare are not carnal but mighty in God for pulling down strongholds." These strongholds, often manifesting as addictions, negative thoughts, or harmful behaviors, can only be dismantled by the power of Christ's blood. The proclamation of His victory on the cross enables believers to take every thought captive and align it with the obedience of Christ.

One of the most powerful examples of healing through faith is found in the story of the woman with the issue of blood. According to Jewish law, a woman experiencing a continuous flow of blood was considered unclean (Leviticus 15:25-27). This meant she was not allowed to enter the temple, participate in religious ceremonies, or even have normal social interactions. She was ostracized from society, carrying not only the burden of her illness but also the shame and isolation that came with it.

For twelve years, this woman had suffered, spending all her money on doctors who could not heal her (Mark 5:25-26). Yet, despite her suffering, she displayed extraordinary faith when she reached out to touch the hem of Jesus' garment. Matthew 9:20-22, Mark 5:25-34, and Luke 8:43-49 all recount this moment of desperate faith. She believed that if she could just touch Jesus' clothes, she would be healed. And in an instant, she was. The power of Jesus' blood and His divine presence immediately restored her. Jesus, sensing that power had gone out from Him, turned and asked, "Who touched me?" His disciples, puzzled by the question, pointed out that many people were crowding around Him. But Jesus knew this was different. The woman, trembling, admitted what she had done. Instead of rebuking her, Jesus affirmed her faith, saying in Mark 5:34, "Daughter, your faith has made you well. Go in peace and be healed of your affliction."

This miracle was more than just a physical healing – it was also a spiritual and social restoration. By healing her, Jesus reversed the Jewish law that declared her unclean. His sacrifice on the cross would later fulfill and surpass the Law, showing that faith in Him brings healing, redemption, and restoration. This event foreshadowed the ultimate power of His blood to cleanse and heal all who come to Him in faith.

In spiritual warfare, the act of confessing and proclaiming the blood of Jesus is both powerful and transformative. Hebrews 10:23 encourages believers to "hold fast the confession of our hope without wavering." As Pastor Derek Prince aptly stated, "Confessing strengthens believing, and believing strengthens confessing." This reciprocal relationship between faith and confession underpins the use of the blood in spiritual battles, ensuring that believers remain steadfast and unshaken, even in the face of adversity.

Personal testimony often serves as a profound illustration of the power of the blood of Jesus in spiritual warfare. One such example involves a believer trapped in fear, mental confusion, and spiritual bondage. Through prayer and the consistent application of the blood in communion, this individual experienced a transformation. The fog of fear lifted, clarity returned, and the chains of the past were broken. This story demonstrates that when the blood of Jesus is applied with faith, it becomes a force for deliverance, healing, and restoration.

The blood of Jesus also plays a pivotal role in the court of heaven, where spiritual matters are addressed before God. As Hebrews 9:24 explains, "For Christ has not entered the holy places made with hands, which are copies of the true, but into heaven itself, now to appear in the presence of God for us." Jesus, as our great High Priest, intercedes for believers, using His blood as a defense against accusations from the enemy. This intercession ensures that the devil's plans are rendered ineffective, providing believers with spiritual security.

In the context of spiritual warfare, the words we speak and the attitudes we hold carry significant weight. Confession and thanksgiving are essential in activating the protective power of the blood of Jesus. Hebrews 4:14 highlights this truth: "Seeing then that we have a great High Priest who has passed through the heavens, Jesus the Son of God, let us hold fast our confession." This verse underscores the importance of proclaiming our faith boldly and with gratitude, aligning our hearts with the victory already won through Christ. Additionally, 1 Peter 5:9 encourages believers to stand fast in opposing the devil, as all believers are: "Resist him, standing firm in the faith, because you know that the family of believers throughout the world is undergoing the same kind of sufferings."

Proclaiming the blood of Jesus in the face of spiritual warfare is not merely a symbolic act but one that resonates powerfully in the spiritual realm. The devil cannot withstand the blood, nor can demonic forces resist its authority. When believers declare, "Through the blood of Jesus, I am justified, cleansed, and set apart for God," they are not only stating a truth but actively participating in their deliverance. This act of faith disarms the enemy and reinforces the believer's position as a child of God.

The blood of Jesus not only cleanses and redeems but also leaves a distinct mark on the believer, both internally and externally. Internally, the blood marks us as God's own by bringing salvation, redemption, justification, sanctification, and the promise of eternal life. These are transformative effects that change the very core of our identity. We are no longer slaves to sin but sons and daughters of God. The blood purifies our hearts and gives us peace with God, sealing us with His Spirit for the day of redemption.

Externally, the blood is a visible sign in the spirit realm. Demons recognize those who are covered by the blood. Blood acts as a barrier against demonic attacks, spiritual oppression, and the schemes of the enemy. It offers divine protection, just as it did for the Israelites in Egypt when the destroyer passed over the blood-marked doors. This outward mark is not seen by human eyes but is powerful and undeniable in the spiritual world. By applying the blood through proclamation, believers reinforce both the inward transformation and the outward protection that Jesus provided through His sacrifice. The blood becomes a banner of victory, guarding and guiding the life of the faithful.

Practical applications of the blood in spiritual warfare include prayers for protection over families, homes, and personal well-being. For instance, proclaiming the blood of Jesus over one's household can serve as a spiritual barrier against attacks, ensuring peace and safety. Similarly, taking communion with a heart of faith and repentance symbolizes the internalization of Christ's sacrifice, strengthening the believer spiritually and aligning them with God's will.

Communion, in particular, holds a unique place in spiritual warfare. As believers partake of the bread and wine, representing Christ's body and blood, they engage in a tangible act of faith that reinforces their victory over sin and darkness. Personal experiences often testify to the miraculous outcomes of this practice. One story recounts how a believer, plagued by fear and confusion, found freedom and clarity through the daily act of taking communion. This simple yet profound act became a channel through which the power of the blood transformed their life.

The blood of Jesus also breaks generational curses and dismantles spiritual strongholds. Bondages such as addictions, negative thought patterns, or harmful behaviors often have deep roots, but the power of the blood can sever these ties completely. John 8:36 declares, "So if the Son sets you free, you will be free indeed." By applying the blood in faith, believers can break free from the chains of sin and live in the fullness of Christ's victory.

The power of the blood extends to protecting believers from the works of darkness. As 1 John 1:7 states, "But if we walk in the light, as He is in the light, we have fellowship with one another, and the blood of Jesus Christ His Son cleanses us from all sin." This cleansing is not limited to forgiveness but includes purification and the ability to resist the devil's schemes. Through prayer, faith, and proclamation, believers activate the blood's protective power, ensuring that no weapon formed against them shall prosper.

The blood of Jesus serves as a shield in spiritual battles, a weapon that defends against the enemy's attacks while reinforcing the believer's identity in Christ. This powerful truth calls Christians to live boldly, proclaiming the victory of the cross and walking in the freedom it provides. Whether in personal struggles or larger spiritual conflicts, the blood remains an ever-present source of strength, cleansing, and protection for those who call upon it.

The power of the blood of Jesus in spiritual warfare not only equips believers to stand against the forces of darkness but also ensures their victory by aligning their actions with the authority of Christ. Beyond defense, the blood empowers believers to reclaim territory lost to the enemy, dismantle spiritual barriers, and break the chains of oppression that often linger in daily life. This active participation in the spiritual realm transforms how believers approach challenges, creating a foundation of faith, courage, and triumph.

A central aspect of engaging in spiritual warfare is understanding the heavenly courts and their role in the battle against evil. As Hebrews 12:24 explains, the blood of Jesus "speaks a better word than the blood of Abel." While Abel's blood cried out for justice, Jesus' blood advocates for mercy, redemption, and victory in the spiritual realm. The court of heaven operates as a place where accusations from Satan are silenced, and believers' cases are defended by the intercession of Christ. This advocacy, empowered by His blood, nullifies the plans of the enemy and affirms the believer's standing in righteousness.

In spiritual warfare, believers can participate in this heavenly process by invoking the blood of Jesus in their prayers and proclamations. This act mirrors the work of Jesus as the High Priest, who continually intercedes for humanity. Through declarations such as "By the blood of Jesus, I am redeemed and set free," believers join their voices with the victorious proclamation of Christ in heaven, amplifying its effect in the spiritual and physical realms.

The blood of Jesus is uniquely powerful in breaking demonic strongholds. These strongholds – whether generational curses, persistent sin, or spiritual oppression – are dismantled through faith and the application of the blood. Personal testimonies reveal the transformative impact of this truth. One believer shared a story of freedom from years of addiction and guilt after fervently applying the blood of Jesus in prayer. By consistently declaring the authority of the blood over their life and committing to live in alignment with God's word, they experienced lasting deliverance.

Breaking spiritual strongholds also involves understanding and addressing their root causes. Many bondages, such as those related to fear, lust, or bitterness, stem from unaddressed spiritual vulnerabilities. In John 8:34-36, Jesus addresses the concept of spiritual slavery: "Very truly I tell you, everyone who sins is a slave to sin… So if the Son sets you free, you will be free indeed." By applying the blood of Jesus and renouncing the lies of the enemy, believers can sever the chains of spiritual bondage and step into the freedom that Christ provides.

Practical steps in spiritual warfare often begin with prayer and the proclamation of the blood's power. These declarations align the believer's actions with biblical truths and call upon the authority of Christ's sacrifice. For example, proclaiming the blood of Jesus over one's mind can guard against intrusive thoughts and anxiety, while applying the blood to a specific situation or relationship can break the influence of demonic interference. Each proclamation serves as both a declaration of faith and an act of spiritual resistance.

The act of applying the blood of Jesus extends beyond personal protection to encompass families, homes, and communities. Praying over a household, for instance, invokes divine protection against spiritual attacks, creating a sanctuary of peace and safety. Many believers report tangible changes in their environment after consistently covering their homes with the blood of Jesus, including a sense of calm, unity, and spiritual clarity. This practice reflects the principles of Exodus 12:23, where the blood of the Passover lamb on the doorposts protected the Israelites from the destroyer.

Spiritual warfare also requires perseverance and boldness. Ephesians 6:13 instructs believers to "take up the whole armor of God," which includes the shield of faith and the sword of the Spirit. The blood of Jesus complements these spiritual tools, serving as the foundation of the believer's authority and strength. Faith in His sacrifice ensures that no attack of the enemy can prevail, while the Word of God, spoken boldly in conjunction with the blood, dismantles lies and defeats darkness.

In combating spiritual attacks, it is essential to recognize the tactics of the enemy. Satan often operates through deception, planting seeds of doubt, fear, and discouragement. By proclaiming the blood of Jesus, believers confront these lies with the truth of Christ's victory. As Revelation 12:11 states, "They triumphed over him by the blood of the Lamb and by the word of their testimony." This triumph is not passive but active, requiring believers to engage in faith-filled actions that affirm their position in Christ.

The power of the blood is also evident in its ability to heal and restore. Just as it cleanses sin, it brings renewal to areas of life affected by spiritual wounds. Whether healing from trauma, releasing bitterness, or overcoming grief, the blood of Jesus offers a pathway to wholeness. Many personal testimonies recount miraculous transformations following the intentional application of the blood in prayer. These accounts serve as reminders that Christ's sacrifice was not only for salvation but for complete restoration.

Communion plays a vital role in maintaining the believer's connection to the power of the blood. By partaking of the bread and wine, believers reaffirm their faith in Jesus' sacrifice and its ongoing impact. This sacred act strengthens the believer's spirit, reinforcing their authority in spiritual battles. Regularly engaging in communion with a repentant and humble heart allows the blood's power to permeate every aspect of life, from personal struggles to intercessory prayers for others.

Another dimension of spiritual warfare is the breaking of curses and generational strongholds through the blood of Jesus. Curses, whether spoken, inherited, or self-inflicted, lose their power when confronted with the authority of Christ's sacrifice. Galatians 3:13 declares, "Christ redeemed us from the curse of the law by becoming a curse for us." By invoking the blood, believers can cancel these curses and replace them with blessings, ensuring that their lives and futures align with God's promises.

Finally, spiritual warfare aligns with the heavenly realm, where Jesus continues His intercessory work on behalf of believers. His blood, shed on the cross and now present in the heavenly courts, serves as an eternal testimony of victory. This alignment bridges the earthly and spiritual dimensions, allowing believers to operate with the authority of heaven in their daily lives. By invoking the blood in faith, they partner with Christ's ongoing mission, bringing light into darkness and establishing God's kingdom on earth.

The power of the blood of Jesus is unmatched, offering protection, deliverance, and restoration in the midst of spiritual warfare. Whether breaking strongholds, defeating demonic attacks, or securing peace, the blood remains an ever-present source of victory for those who call upon it. Through prayer, proclamation, and faith, believers can fully access the transformative power of Christ's sacrifice, living as overcomers in a world often overshadowed by spiritual challenges.

Chapter Five:
Healing Through The Blood

God shows us his love, grace and mercy by shedding his blood on the cross. God is a just God, judge, and advocate. His advocacy for us was demonstrated by Jesus on the Cross.

(Monika Starova)

The blood of Jesus Christ stands as the cornerstone of spiritual healing, offering restoration to the body, mind, and soul. His sacrifice not only reconciles humanity to God but also provides a pathway to wholeness in every aspect of life. Through His stripes, His suffering, and His shed blood, Jesus fulfilled the divine promise of healing, as declared in Isaiah 53:5.

The process of healing begins with the recognition of Christ's sacrifice and the redemptive power of His blood. At the hands of Roman soldiers, Jesus was scourged with a whip that tore into His back, a brutal act of suffering that carried profound spiritual significance. Matthew 27:26 recounts this event, where He was scourged before being led to the cross. The physical torment He endured redeemed humanity from the bondage of sickness and disease. His blood, shed during this agonizing process, became the means through which believers are made whole.

The atonement achieved through the blood of Jesus is twofold. As Pastor Benny Hinn explains, the atonement in front of the cross represents salvation for the soul, while the atonement behind the cross signifies physical healing. This dual aspect of Christ's work is further emphasized by Derek Prince, who noted that Jesus' ministry began and ended in perfection, with His sacrificial death bringing His mission to completion. The declaration "It is finished" (John 19:30) confirmed that the work of redemption and healing was perfectly accomplished.

Faith plays a central role in activating the healing power of Jesus' blood. Throughout His ministry, Jesus emphasized the necessity of faith in receiving healing. In Mark 9:23, He proclaimed, "If you can believe, all things are possible to him who believes." Faith is not merely intellectual assent but an active trust in the promises of God. The woman with the issue of blood (Mark 5:25-34) exemplified this principle. Despite her long-standing illness, she believed that touching the hem of Jesus' garment would bring healing. Her faith made her whole, and Jesus confirmed this by saying, "Daughter, your faith has made you well."

Healing through the blood of Jesus extends beyond the physical realm to encompass mental and emotional restoration. The challenges of modern life, including depression, anxiety, and addiction, often create spiritual strongholds that can feel insurmountable. However, the blood of Jesus breaks these chains, offering freedom and renewal.

Through faith in His blood, believers can overcome the darkest struggles, finding peace and restoration in Christ.

The transformative power of Jesus' blood is rooted in its ability to reverse the effects of sin, including sickness and suffering. From the moment Adam and Eve disobeyed God in the Garden of Eden, humanity was subjected to the consequences of sin, including physical illness and spiritual separation. Genesis 3:16-19 describes the curse that entered the world through Adam's fall, bringing pain, toil, and death. Yet Jesus came to redeem humanity from this curse, bearing the weight of sin and its consequences on the cross. Galatians 3:13 affirms.

The ministry of Jesus on earth demonstrated God's desire for healing and restoration. Luke 4:18 captures the essence of His mission: "The Spirit of the Lord is upon Me because He has anointed Me to preach the gospel to the poor; He has sent Me to heal the brokenhearted, to proclaim liberty to the captives, and recovery of sight to the blind." Through countless miracles, Jesus displayed His authority over sickness and death. From healing Peter's mother-in-law of a fever (Matthew 8:14-15) to raising Jairus's daughter (Luke 8:49-56), His works revealed the compassionate heart of God.

Jesus also empowered His disciples to continue His healing ministry. In Matthew 10:1, He gave them authority over unclean spirits and the ability to heal all kinds of sickness and disease. This commissioning extended beyond the apostles to all who believed in Him. Mark 16:17-18 confirms this promise: "And these signs will follow those who believe: In My name, they will cast out demons... they will lay hands on the sick, and they will recover." Through the Holy Spirit, believers today are equipped to participate in the healing work of Christ, bringing restoration to others through prayer and faith.

The connection between spiritual and physical healing is evident in the stories of Jesus' miracles. In Luke 10:9, He instructed His disciples to "heal the sick who are there and tell them, 'The kingdom of God has come near to you.'" This directive underscores the holistic nature of God's kingdom, where salvation and healing go hand in hand. The healing of the paralytic man in Matthew 9:1-8 highlights this truth. Before addressing the man's physical condition, Jesus forgave his sins, demonstrating that spiritual restoration is foundational to physical healing.

The power of Jesus' blood in healing is not confined to the biblical narrative but continues to manifest in the lives of believers today. Personal testimonies of healing provide compelling evidence of this truth. One woman, burdened by chronic illness and despair, experienced a miraculous recovery after consistently praying and declaring the healing power of Jesus' blood. Another individual, trapped in the grip of addiction, found freedom and renewal through faith in Christ's sacrifice. These stories testify to the enduring impact of His blood in bringing wholeness to those who trust in Him.

Faith-filled prayers and proclamations are essential tools for accessing the healing power of Jesus' blood. Isaiah 53:5 serves as a cornerstone verse for such declarations: "By His wounds, we are healed." When believers speak this truth over their lives and situations, they align their faith with God's promises, creating an atmosphere for miracles to occur. Proclaiming the blood of Jesus in prayer reinforces the reality of His victory over sickness and affirms the believer's trust in His healing power.

The concept of "Dunamis," a Greek word describing the supernatural power of God, underscores the miraculous nature of healing through the blood of Jesus. This divine power, mentioned in passages such as Acts 1:8 and 2 Timothy 1:7, enables believers to overcome limitations and experience breakthroughs that defy human understanding. The presence of Dunamis within every Christian is a testament to the transformative work of the Holy Spirit, who empowers believers to walk in health, freedom, and victory.

Healing through the blood of Jesus is also connected to the renewal of the mind and spirit. Romans 12:2 encourages believers to "be transformed by the renewing of your mind." This renewal, made possible by Christ's sacrifice, breaks the cycle of negative thought patterns and brings clarity and peace. By applying the blood of Jesus in daily prayer and meditation, believers can experience a profound shift in their mental and emotional well-being, finding strength and hope in the midst of life's challenges.

The first step in accessing this healing is to approach God with a heart of faith and repentance. Taking communion, for example, serves as a powerful reminder of Christ's sacrifice and its ongoing impact. When believers partake of the bread and wine, they affirm their trust in His broken body and shed blood as the source of their healing. This act of faith not only reinforces their spiritual connection to Christ but also creates an opportunity for His healing power to flow into their lives.

The healing power of Jesus' blood is not limited to physical restoration but extends to mental and spiritual renewal, addressing the deepest wounds and struggles faced by humanity. Through His sacrifice, Jesus offers a complete healing that encompasses every area of life, breaking chains of addiction, depression, and fear, and transforming individuals into new creations in Him.

One of the profound aspects of Christ's healing is its ability to break the strongholds of the mind. Many individuals wrestle with internal battles – negative thought patterns, anxiety, and destructive habits – that seem impossible to overcome. However, the blood of Jesus provides the power to renew the mind and bring freedom from these afflictions. Romans 8:6 captures this truth: "The mind governed by the flesh is death, but the mind governed by the Spirit is life and peace." By applying the blood of Jesus and surrendering to the Holy Spirit, believers can experience the renewal of their thoughts and a transformation in their mental well-being.

The story of the woman with the issue of blood (Mark 5:25-34) illustrates how faith in Jesus' power can bring about not only physical healing but also emotional restoration. For twelve years, she suffered not only from her illness but also from the social isolation and shame it caused. Yet her act of faith – reaching out to touch Jesus' garment – resulted in complete healing. Jesus' response, "Your faith has made you well," highlights the integral connection between faith and healing. This encounter demonstrates that the blood of Jesus can address the physical, emotional, and social wounds that weigh on individuals.

Breaking the chains of addiction is another area where the blood of Jesus brings powerful healing. Addictions – whether to substances, behaviors, or thought patterns – often enslave individuals, creating a cycle of guilt and despair. John 8:34-36 sheds light on this struggle: "Very truly I tell you, everyone who sins is a slave to sin... So if the Son sets you free, you will be free indeed." Through the blood of Jesus, believers can find deliverance from these chains, as His sacrifice provides the strength to overcome and the grace to start anew.

Practical application of the blood of Jesus in daily life is a crucial aspect of accessing its healing power. One effective approach is through faith-filled prayer and proclamation. By declaring verses such as Isaiah 53:5, believers align their faith with the promises of God, speaking life and restoration into their circumstances. These declarations are not merely words but acts of faith that invite the Holy Spirit to work in and through them, breaking strongholds and bringing healing.

Communion is another powerful way to connect with the healing power of Jesus' blood. This sacred practice symbolizes the body and blood of Christ, broken and shed for the healing of humanity. When believers partake of communion with faith and repentance, they internalize the reality of His sacrifice, allowing His healing power to flow into their lives. One testimony shared the story of a woman who, through daily communion and prayer, experienced healing from fear and confusion, finding clarity and peace after years of struggle.

Faith is a fundamental element in receiving healing through the blood of Jesus. Hebrews 11:1 defines faith as "the substance of things hoped for, the evidence of things not seen." It is through this faith that believers access the promises of God, including healing. The gospels recount numerous instances where Jesus emphasized the role of faith in miracles. For example, in Matthew 9:27-30, two blind men approached Jesus, crying out for mercy. He responded, "According to your faith let it be to you," and their sight was restored. These stories remind believers that faith is not just a passive belief but an active trust in God's ability to heal and restore.

The role of faith is further illustrated in the connection between spiritual and physical healing. Jesus often healed individuals by addressing their spiritual condition first, as seen in the story of the paralytic man in Matthew 9:2-7. Before healing his physical ailment, Jesus declared, "Your sins are forgiven." This act demonstrated that spiritual restoration is foundational to physical healing. By aligning their hearts with God through repentance and faith, believers open themselves to the transformative power of Christ's blood.

WHY THE SHEDDING OF THE BLOOD?

The healing brought by the blood of Jesus is not limited to individuals but extends to families and communities. By covering loved ones in prayer and proclaiming the blood over their lives, believers can invite God's protection and restoration into their homes. Many testimonies recount how families experienced reconciliation, peace, and healing after intentionally applying the blood of Jesus in prayer. This practice reflects the principle seen in Exodus 12:7, where the Israelites marked their doorframes with the blood of the lamb for protection. Today, believers can spiritually apply the blood to their families, trusting in its power to safeguard and restore.

The power of Jesus' blood is also evident in its ability to heal deep emotional wounds, such as those caused by trauma, grief, and rejection. Psalm 34:18 assures us, "The Lord is close to the brokenhearted and saves those who are crushed in spirit." Through His sacrifice, Jesus bore not only the physical pain of the cross but also the weight of humanity's emotional suffering. By surrendering these wounds to Him and claiming His healing, believers can experience a profound sense of peace and renewal.

Spiritual healing is another dimension of the restorative work of Christ's blood. Sin creates a barrier between humanity and God, leading to spiritual death. However, the blood of Jesus removes this barrier, reconciling believers to God and restoring their spiritual health. Ephesians 1:7 affirms, "In Him we have redemption through His blood, the forgiveness of sins, in accordance with the riches of God's grace." This forgiveness is the foundation of spiritual healing, enabling believers to live in freedom and intimacy with their Creator.

One significant aspect of spiritual healing is the renewal of the believer's identity. Through the blood of Jesus, individuals are no longer defined by their past failures or struggles but are given a new identity as children of God. 2 Corinthians 5:17 declares, "Therefore, if anyone is in Christ, he is a new creation; old things have passed away; behold, all things have become new." This transformation empowers believers to walk in confidence and purpose, free from the shame and guilt that once held them captive.

The healing power of Jesus' blood also has implications for the Church as a whole. As the body of Christ, the Church is called to be a place of healing and restoration, reflecting the ministry of Jesus. By proclaiming the blood of Jesus and exercising faith, believers can bring hope and healing to those in their communities. Whether through intercessory prayer, laying on of hands, or acts of compassion, the Church can serve as a conduit for God's healing power.

Ultimately, the healing provided by the blood of Jesus is a testament to God's love and mercy. His desire is for His people to be whole in every area of life – physically, mentally, and spiritually. By faith, believers can access this healing and experience the abundant life that Jesus promised in John 10:10: "I have come that they may have life, and that they may have it more abundantly." This promise serves as a reminder that God's healing is not only a future hope but a present reality available to all who trust in Him.

Chapter Six:
The Communion: The Power Of The Bread And The Cup

We, as human beings, have the privilege and the blessings to be covered daily with the blood of Jesus. The blood of Jesus and the proclamation of the word of God give us strength, protection, and victory in our daily lives.

(Monika Starova)

In Catholicism and Orthodox Christianity, the Eucharist is considered a sacrament, a sacred and essential part of worship that holds deep spiritual significance. However, Protestant traditions do not universally recognize it as a sacrament but rather as an ordinance or symbolic practice. The sacrament of communion, also known as the Lord's Supper or the Holy Eucharist, stands as one of the most profound practices in Christian faith. For Catholics and Orthodox Christians, it is more than a symbolic act; it is viewed as a means of receiving grace and spiritual nourishment. This sacred act is a central sacrament in Christian tradition, approached with reverence, preparation, and awe. It signifies spiritual nourishment, unity with Christ, and solidarity among believers. It commemorates Jesus Christ's sacrifice, embodying the powerful symbolism of His body and blood. By taking the bread and the cup, believers partake in a spiritual experience that connects them to the redemptive work of Christ and reinforces their faith in the transformative power of His blood.

The foundation of communion lies in the words of Jesus during the Last Supper, as recorded in Luke 22:14-21. Jesus shared a meal with His disciples, breaking bread and offering wine as symbols of His body and blood, which would soon be given for the salvation of humanity. At the Last Supper, Jesus not only shared bread and wine with His disciples but also gave them a sacred command: "This is my body given for you; do this in remembrance of me." This instruction became the foundation of the Eucharistic celebration, a profound act of remembrance and devotion. He also added, "This cup is the new covenant in my blood, which is poured out for you." These words established communion as a continual reminder of Christ's sacrifice and the new covenant formed through His blood.

The bread and the cup symbolize the essence of Christ's atonement. The bread, representing His body, speaks of the physical suffering He endured to bear humanity's sins. The cup, symbolizing His blood, represents the life-giving power of His sacrifice. Leviticus 17:11 underscores this truth: "For the life of the flesh is in the blood, and I have given it to you upon the altar to make atonement for your souls." Through the act of communion, pastors, priests, and believers affirm their faith in the efficacy of Christ's atoning work.

Communion is not merely a ritual but a declaration of faith. By participating, believers proclaim the Lord's death until He comes again (1 Corinthians 11:26). This act of faith is an outward expression of an inward reality – the believer's trust in the sufficiency of Christ's sacrifice. As I explain, "By the blood of Christ and the word of my testimony, the proclamation of the word of God by faith and boldness, when we are weak, in Jesus we are strong. His blood brings us to the throne of grace in front of the Father to hear our prayers and communicate with us."

The historical and theological importance of communion is deeply rooted in the church's traditions. From the earliest days of Christianity, the Lord's Supper was observed as a central act of worship. It was a means of remembering Christ's sacrifice, fostering unity among believers, and participating in the spiritual blessings of the new covenant. The early church fathers emphasized the profound mystery of communion, viewing it as a sacrament that unites the believer with Christ and His body, the Church. This perspective is particularly emphasized in Catholic and Orthodox teachings, where the Eucharist is believed to be a real participation in Christ's sacrifice, rather than merely a symbolic remembrance.

The practice of communion also serves as a reminder of God's covenant with humanity. In the Old Testament, covenants were often sealed with blood, symbolizing the seriousness and permanence of the agreement. Genesis 3:21 illustrates the first instance of a blood covenant when God made garments of skin to cover Adam and Eve's nakedness after their sin. This act of grace foreshadowed the ultimate covering of sin through the blood of Christ. As Jesus said during the Last Supper, "This cup is the new covenant in my blood." This statement signifies the fulfillment of the Old Testament covenants and the establishment of a new and everlasting covenant through His sacrifice.

Taking communion is not only a remembrance of Christ's sacrifice but also an act that activates spiritual protection and healing. The blood of Jesus has the power to break every curse, cleanse sin, and bring wholeness to the body and soul. By drinking the cup, believers symbolically apply the blood of Christ to their lives, declaring its power over sin, sickness, and the forces of darkness. In John 6:50-51, Jesus says, "This is the bread that comes down out of heaven, so that one may eat of it and not die. I am the living bread that came down out of heaven; if anyone eats of this bread, he will live forever; and the bread also which I will give for the life of the world is My flesh."

The spiritual significance of the bread and cup is further amplified by their role in renewing the believer's connection to the power of Christ's blood. Communion serves as a tangible reminder of the believer's identity in Christ and the victory won through His sacrifice. By partaking in the bread and wine, believers reaffirm their faith in the cleansing and redeeming power of His blood, drawing strength and renewal from this divine connection. Partaking in the Holy Eucharist is a deeply symbolic act, signifying spiritual nourishment, intimate communion with Christ, and unity with fellow believers. It represents a life-giving sacrament that fosters profound connection and shared identity among members of faith.

Communion also plays a role in spiritual warfare. The act of taking the bread and cup is a declaration of victory over the enemy, a reminder that Christ's blood has already defeated Satan and his forces. Through communion, believers align themselves with this victory, proclaiming their freedom from the power of sin and darkness.

The practice of communion is not limited to earthly worship but also reflects a heavenly reality. As Jesus intercedes for believers in the heavenly courts, the symbolism of His blood continues to hold power.

Hebrews 9:24 reveals that Christ entered heaven itself to appear for us in God's presence. His ongoing intercession and the eternal significance of His blood ensure that the blessings of the new covenant remain accessible to believers. Communion serves as a bridge between this heavenly reality and the earthly experience of God's grace. When believers partake in the Eucharist, they encounter the living Christ in a tangible and intimate way, experiencing His sacrificial love, redemption, and grace in a profound manner.

In addition to its spiritual significance, communion has practical implications for the believer's daily life. It encourages self-examination and repentance, fostering a heart posture of humility and gratitude. As 1 Corinthians 11:28 advises, "Let a man examine himself, and so let him eat of the bread and drink of the cup." This act of introspection allows believers to approach the table of the Lord with reverence and faith, ready to receive the blessings of communion.

The transformative power of communion is evident in the testimonies of believers who have experienced healing, deliverance, and restoration through this sacred practice. One example is the story of a woman who, after years of emotional and spiritual turmoil, began taking communion daily with faith and repentance. Through this act, she experienced freedom from fear and a renewed sense of peace and purpose. Her testimony illustrates the profound impact of communion as a means of applying the blood of Jesus to one's life.

Communion is also a source of unity within the body of Christ. As believers partake of the bread and cup together, they are reminded of their shared identity in Christ and their role as members of His body. This unity transcends cultural, social, and denominational boundaries, reflecting the universal nature of the new covenant. 1 Corinthians 10:16 affirms this truth: "The cup of blessing that we bless, is it not a participation in the blood of Christ? The bread that we break, is it not a participation in the body of Christ?"

Communion represents a unique intersection between the earthly and the heavenly, a sacred act that bridges time and space. The act of taking communion is not confined to earthly realms but mirrors a spiritual reality in heaven. In Revelation 19:9, we find reference to the "marriage supper of the Lamb," a celebration that symbolizes the ultimate communion between Christ and His bride, the Church. This heavenly feast demonstrates that communion is an eternal practice, uniting believers with Christ both now and forever.

When Jesus instituted the Lord's Supper, He emphasized the covenantal nature of the bread and wine, stating in Luke 22:19-20, "This is My body, which is given for you; do this in remembrance of Me. This cup is the new covenant in My blood, which is poured out for you." His words highlighted the sacrificial essence of communion, drawing a direct line from the Old Testament covenants, sealed with the blood of animals, to the New Covenant, established through His own blood. This act was a declaration of the fulfillment of centuries of divine promises and a call for believers to remember and participate in the new covenant continually.

The bread and cup are not mere symbols but spiritual tools that carry profound power when received in faith. The bread represents the broken body of Christ, reminding believers of the suffering He endured to bring healing and restoration. Each time the bread is taken, believers proclaim the reality of Christ's physical sacrifice and its implications for their health and wholeness.

Similarly, the cup signifies the shed blood of Jesus, a reminder of the price paid for humanity's redemption. Hebrews 9:22 states, "Without the shedding of blood, there is no forgiveness." Drinking from the cup is a powerful declaration of faith in the cleansing and life-giving power of Jesus' blood. It affirms the believer's participation in the covenant and their acceptance of the grace and forgiveness it brings.

The spiritual significance of communion is further amplified through its practical application in the believer's life. When taken with reverence and faith, communion serves as a source of spiritual strength and renewal. It reminds believers of the victory already won through Christ and equips them to face challenges with confidence. By remembering Christ's sacrifice, believers are also encouraged to live sacrificially, extending grace and love to others as a reflection of the love they have received.

Communion also activates spiritual protection. In the Old Testament, the blood of the Passover lamb, applied to the doorframes of the Israelites' homes, protected them from the destroyer (Exodus 12:7, 13). Similarly, the blood of Jesus, represented by the cup, serves as a shield against spiritual attacks for believers today. Through the Holy Eucharist, believers are strengthened to resist the temptations and challenges of a fallen world, finding grace and power in their communion with Christ. By partaking in communion, believers declare their trust in Christ's sacrifice as the ultimate source of safety and deliverance from the enemy.

Furthermore, communion offers a pathway to healing. As 1 Corinthians 11:29-30 warns, those who take communion "without discerning the body of Christ" risk bringing judgment upon themselves, and for this reason, "many are weak and ill, and some have died." Conversely, partaking of communion with faith and understanding allows believers to access the healing power of Christ's sacrifice. The act of taking the bread and cup with a repentant heart aligns the believer with the spiritual reality of wholeness and restoration made possible through the cross.

The communal aspect of the Lord's Supper highlights the importance of reconciliation and unity within the body of Christ. Before participating in communion, believers are encouraged to examine their hearts and seek reconciliation with others (Matthew 5:23-24). This practice ensures that the unity symbolized by the bread and cup is reflected in the relationships among those who partake. By addressing interpersonal conflicts and fostering forgiveness, believers honor the covenant of grace that Christ established through His blood.

Personal testimonies further illustrate the transformative power of communion. One such story involves a man burdened by chronic illness and despair. Through consistent participation in communion, combined with faith-filled declarations of Isaiah 53:5, he experienced physical healing and spiritual renewal. His story is a testament to the reality that the bread and cup are not merely symbolic but carry a tangible connection to the power of Christ's sacrifice when received in faith.

The importance of faith in communion cannot be overstated. Hebrews 11:6 reminds us that "without faith, it is impossible to please God." When believers approach the Lord's Table with faith, they activate the promises inherent in the covenant. Communion becomes more than a ritual; it becomes a living interaction with the grace and power of God. This act of faith allows believers to experience the fullness of what the bread and cup represent, including forgiveness, healing, and protection.

Communion is also a time for reflection and gratitude. As believers recall the immense price paid by Jesus, they are drawn into a deeper appreciation of His love and mercy. The Lord's Supper is an opportunity to recount the faithfulness of God throughout history and in their own life, fostering a heart of thanksgiving. This posture of gratitude not only honors Christ's sacrifice but also strengthens the believer's relationship with Him.

The act of communion reaches beyond the individual and extends to the collective body of Christ. It is a unifying practice that brings believers together across generations and denominations, reminding them of their shared identity in Christ. As Paul writes in 1 Corinthians 10:17, "Because there is one bread, we who are many are one body, for we all partake of the one bread." This unity reflects the heart of God's plan for His Church, a diverse yet harmonious family joined by the blood of Christ.

In the heavenly realm, the significance of communion is mirrored through Christ's ongoing intercession for believers. Hebrews 7:25 affirms, "He always lives to make intercession for them." This advocacy is a continuation of the covenant established through His blood, a reminder that the power of His sacrifice is both eternal and active. Communion on earth serves as a reflection of this heavenly reality, connecting believers to the divine work of Christ in the spiritual realm.

As the Church awaits the return of Christ, communion serves as both a remembrance of His first coming and a preparation for His second. Revelation 22:17 offers an invitation to all: "The Spirit and the bride say, 'Come.' And let the one who hears say, 'Come.' Let the one who is thirsty come; and let the one who wishes take the free gift of the water of life." The Lord's Supper is a foretaste of the eternal communion believers will share with Christ in His kingdom, a reminder of the hope and glory that lie ahead.

The practice of communion is a sacred act that encapsulates the entirety of the Christian faith. Through the bread and cup, believers proclaim the death, resurrection, and return of Christ, drawing strength and grace from His sacrifice. The Eucharist is a life-giving sacrament, embodying the heart of Christian worship. It provides spiritual nourishment, fosters unity, and serves as a powerful reminder of Christ's sacrifice and His abiding presence among His people. It is a moment of profound spiritual connection, an opportunity to renew their covenant with God and align their lives with His purposes. By approaching the Lord's Table with faith, reverence, and gratitude, believers can experience the transformative power of Christ's blood and the unity of His body, both now and for eternity.

Chapter Seven:
The Power Of Proclamation

There is more power in a little drop of the blood of Jesus than all the legions of satanic beings in the spiritual realm.

(Monika Starova)

The spoken word is an essential tool for believers to access and activate the power of the blood of Jesus in both the spiritual and physical realms. When spoken with faith, words carry authority and bring divine intervention into everyday situations. The Bible emphasizes the impact of our words, declaring in Proverbs 18:21 that "death and life are in the power of the tongue." This profound truth reveals how our spoken declarations can either align us with God's promises or leave us vulnerable to the enemy's schemes. The act of proclaiming the blood of Jesus is a deliberate declaration of faith, an act of spiritual warfare that enforces the victory Christ secured on the cross.

Jesus' crucifixion and the shedding of His blood fulfilled the ultimate plan of redemption for humanity. Through His sacrifice, the curse of sin and death was broken, granting believers access to a life of victory, healing, and divine blessings. Yet, this victory must be enforced through proclamation. Hebrews 4:14 calls believers to "hold fast our confession." This confession is not merely acknowledgment but an active declaration of faith, speaking the truth of God's Word over every situation. Proclamation bridges the gap between what Christ accomplished on the cross and its manifestation in the believer's life.

The practice of proclamation has its foundation in biblical principles. From the creation account, where God spoke the universe into existence, to the teachings of Jesus about faith-filled words, Scripture consistently highlights the transformative power of the spoken word. Mark 11:23 illustrates this clearly: "If anyone says to this mountain, 'Be lifted up and thrown into the sea,' and does not doubt in his heart but believes that what he says will happen, it will be done for him." Similarly, when believers proclaim the power of the blood of Jesus, they are speaking life, healing, and victory into their circumstances. The Word of God, combined with faith-filled proclamation, releases the transformative power of His blood.

Daily proclamations of the blood of Jesus have the power to bring spiritual protection and to address various challenges in life. For instance, a believer may declare, "By the blood of Jesus, my family is protected from all harm. No weapon formed against us shall prosper." Such proclamations are not mere words but spiritual acts that establish divine protection over loved ones. The power of proclamation also extends to breaking spiritual strongholds. Declaring, "By the blood of Jesus, I am set free from the power of sin and the schemes of the enemy," reinforces the victory of Christ and breaks the enemy's hold over the believer's life. Revelation 12:11 affirms this truth. The combination of the blood and the believer's spoken testimony creates a powerful defense against the enemy's attacks.

∗∗

I passionately believe that proclaiming the effects of Jesus' blood is not just important – it is absolutely essential for those effects to be activated in our lives. The blood of Jesus holds unmatched power, but its benefits are not automatic. They must be spoken aloud, declared with faith and conviction. It's not enough to simply know about the power of the blood – you have to declare it with your mouth. Proclamation is a spiritual weapon. It brings breakthrough, victory, and transformation in our everyday walk with God.

I often compare this to the Passover in Exodus. The Israelites didn't just believe in the power of the lamb's blood – they had to apply it to their doorposts to be protected. In the same way, I must proclaim the blood of Jesus over my life. I say things like, "I overcome the devil by the blood of the Lamb and the word of my testimony," or "Thank you, Jesus, because I'm in the light." These are not just words for emergencies or church gatherings – they are declarations I make daily over my family, my home, my health, my finances, and every spiritual battle I face.

I know that this kind of verbal declaration releases the power of the blood into every area of life. When I proclaim the blood of Jesus, I release divine protection from evil, provision for every need, healing in my body, and victory in spiritual warfare. The enemy trembles when he hears the blood proclaimed with authority. But if I stay silent, if I don't speak with faith, I leave the door open. I always say, "If you don't say it, it won't work." God provides the blood, but we must apply it through our faith and our proclamation. This is how we partner with God to see His power released in our lives.

**

Faith is the essential ingredient that gives power to proclamation. Without faith, words are empty and lack spiritual authority. Hebrews 10:23 emphasizes this connection. Faith transforms proclamation into a spiritual weapon, aligning the believer's words with God's promises and unleashing divine power. One powerful testimony demonstrates how a believer who faced significant professional challenges turned to proclamation in faith. A doctor who was unfairly removed from an essential platform for his clinic prayed using declarations of the blood of Jesus. Within 48 hours, his situation was miraculously resolved. This example highlights how faith-filled proclamations can bring about tangible breakthroughs.

The application of the blood of Jesus through proclamation is particularly effective in resisting jealousy, envy, and other spiritual attacks, often referred to as the "evil eye." These forces seek to hinder progress, create strife, and sow discord. A daily prayer for protection might include, "I apply the blood of Jesus over my life, my family, and my work. I declare that no weapon formed against me shall prosper, and every plan of the enemy is defeated." This simple yet powerful declaration establishes a spiritual shield that repels such attacks and keeps the believer rooted in God's promises.

A powerful example of the impact of proclamation involves a doctor who faced a significant obstacle in his business. He owned a private clinic that relied heavily on Google advertisements for visibility. One day, he was informed by a Google representative that his clinic's advertisements had been removed due to non-compliance with their policies. In his frustration, he sought guidance, and I encouraged him to pray in the court of heaven, using proclamations that invoked the power of the blood of Jesus. With a repentant and humble heart, he followed the suggested prayers, declaring the authority of Jesus' blood over his situation. Remarkably, within 48 hours, he received notification that his account had been restored, and his advertisements were back online. This testimony underscores the power of proclamation and the advocacy of Jesus as a mediator in the spiritual realm.

The significance of the proclamation is further highlighted in the symbolic imagery of the hyssop, the basin, and the blood. In biblical times, the Israelites applied the blood of the Passover lamb to their doorposts using hyssop, marking their homes as protected by God. Today, believers apply the blood of Jesus through their words, using their testimony and faith as the "hyssop" that activates the power of His blood. Derek Prince taught that the hyssop represents testimony, the basin represents the Word of God, and the blood represents Jesus' sacrifice. Together, these elements form a powerful defense against the enemy's schemes. Psalm 107:2 captures this principle: "Let the redeemed of the Lord say so, whom He has redeemed from the hand of the enemy."

The act of proclamation is not a one-time event but a continual practice. Just as the Israelites had to apply the blood daily during their wilderness journey, believers today must declare the power of Jesus' blood consistently. A daily proclamation might include, "By the blood of Jesus, I am redeemed from the curse of sin. The enemy's plans against me are nullified, and I walk in the blessings of God." Such declarations reinforce the believer's faith and serve as a spiritual reminder of the victory secured through Christ's sacrifice. Faithful proclamation strengthens the believer's connection to the power of Jesus' blood and ensures that His victory remains active in their life.

The connection between proclamation and Jesus' heavenly advocacy further underscores the importance of speaking forth the truth of His blood. Hebrews 9:24 reveals that Christ entered heaven itself to appear for believers in God's presence. Each time a believer declares the power of the blood, they align themselves with Christ's ongoing intercession in the heavenly courts. This divine alignment activates spiritual protection, healing, and deliverance, bringing the reality of Christ's victory into the believer's life.

The sevenfold shedding of Jesus' blood during His passion holds profound significance for proclamation. Each instance of His shed blood represents a specific aspect of redemption and victory that believers can access through their declarations. For example, the blood shed in the Garden of Gethsemane signifies victory over fear and anxiety, while the blood from the crown of thorns symbolizes freedom from mental torment. When believers proclaim, "By the blood of Jesus, I have peace of mind and freedom from anxiety," they tap into the spiritual power represented by these events.

Proclamation is a deliberate act of faith that aligns the believer with God's promises, reinforces their spiritual authority, and brings divine intervention into their circumstances. Through consistent declarations of the power of Jesus' blood, believers establish a spiritual atmosphere of victory and overcome the enemy's schemes. As they proclaim the blood in faith, they access the ongoing heavenly intercession of Christ, unleashing the transformative power of His sacrifice in their lives.

Another of the most profound effects of proclamation is its ability to change personal circumstances. Proclaiming the blood of Jesus over one's health, for instance, aligns the believer with the healing power of His sacrifice. A declaration such as, "By the stripes of Jesus, I am healed," draws from Isaiah 53:5 and serves as a direct invocation of the atonement's promise of physical restoration. For those battling chronic illnesses or sudden afflictions, consistent proclamations reinforce faith in God's healing power, creating an atmosphere where divine intervention can manifest.

In familial relationships, proclamation fosters protection, unity, and peace. Declaring the blood of Jesus over one's household, such as "By the blood of Jesus, my family is covered, protected, and united in Christ," establishes a spiritual boundary that shields against discord, fear, and external influences. Families that regularly engage in such declarations often report an increased sense of harmony and a shared commitment to faith. By proclaiming these truths collectively, households align themselves with God's desire for family unity, making their homes sanctuaries of His presence.

The power of proclamation is equally significant in breaking spiritual barriers and overcoming persistent struggles. For individuals trapped in cycles of addiction, negative thought patterns, or fear, speaking forth the power of Jesus' blood is an act of spiritual defiance against the forces of darkness. One example is declaring, "By the blood of Jesus, I am free from every chain of addiction, and I walk in the liberty of Christ." Such declarations bring to life the promise of John 8:36: "If the Son sets you free, you will be free indeed." The spoken word carries the authority of God's promises, breaking the chains that the enemy uses to bind believers.

Faith remains the cornerstone of effective proclamation. Without faith, declarations lose their potency and fail to invoke the spiritual power they are meant to release. Hebrews 11:1 defines faith as "the substance of things hoped for, the evidence of things not seen." Proclaiming the blood of Jesus with unwavering belief not only strengthens the believer's connection to God's promises but also creates a spiritual atmosphere where miracles become possible. This principle is evident in the story of the Israelites during the Passover. They applied the blood of the lamb to their doorposts as an act of faith, trusting that God would protect them from the destroyer. Today, believers do the same through their words, declaring the power of Jesus' blood as a shield against every attack.

The continuous shedding of Christ's blood, as seen in the vision of His sevenfold sacrifice, offers believers a reservoir of divine power to draw from in every area of life. Each instance of bloodshed – whether in the Garden of Gethsemane, at the whipping post, or on the cross – carries specific spiritual significance. For example, the blood from Jesus' pierced hands symbolizes the restoration of work and productivity. Proclaiming, "By the blood of Jesus, my work is blessed, and everything I touch prospers," taps into this redemptive power, aligning the believer's efforts with God's blessings. Similarly, the blood from His feet signifies authority and dominion over challenges. Declaring, "By the blood of Jesus, I walk in victory and trample every scheme of the enemy," reinforces the believer's spiritual authority.

Proclamation is also deeply tied to spiritual warfare, where spoken declarations serve as offensive and defensive weapons. Ephesians 6:17 describes the Word of God as the "sword of the Spirit," highlighting the active role of spoken truth in overcoming the enemy. Declaring the power of the blood is akin to wielding this sword, cutting through lies, discouragement, and attacks from the enemy. For example, proclaiming, "By the blood of Jesus, I have victory over the enemy, and his plans against me are destroyed," directly counters the schemes of darkness, establishing the believer's authority in Christ.

The act of proclamation is not limited to individual struggles but extends to intercession for others. Believers can declare the power of Jesus' blood over their communities, workplaces, and nations, invoking divine intervention in larger contexts. A prayer such as "By the blood of Jesus, I declare peace and righteousness over my city, and I cancel every plan of the enemy against it" demonstrates the expansive reach of proclamation. Such declarations align with God's heart for restoration and justice, bringing His presence into situations where human efforts alone fall short.

Proclamation also strengthens the believer's relationship with God, fostering intimacy and trust. By declaring the promises of God daily, believers cultivate a habit of speaking His truth over their lives, which in turn deepens their faith. This practice reinforces the understanding that God is both willing and able to fulfill His promises. A simple declaration like, "By the blood of Jesus, I am forgiven, redeemed, and loved by God," serves as a daily reminder of His faithfulness, anchoring the believer in His grace.

The transformative power of proclamation is not confined to the individual believer but extends to the collective body of Christ. When churches and communities engage in unified proclamations, they create a spiritual synergy that amplifies their impact. Declaring the blood of Jesus as a congregation, such as during prayer meetings or worship services, fosters unity and reinforces the shared faith of the group. This collective act serves as a powerful testimony to the world, displaying the strength and victory found in Christ.

The heavenly reality of proclamation is another vital dimension of its power. Hebrews 7:25 reveals that Jesus "always lives to make intercession" for believers, continually advocating for them before the Father. Each time a believer proclaims the power of the blood, they join in this heavenly intercession, aligning their words with the ongoing advocacy of Christ. This alignment activates divine protection, healing, and provision, bringing the reality of heaven into the believer's earthly experience.

Proclamation is not a passive act but a deliberate engagement with the promises of God. It requires faith, persistence, and an understanding of the spiritual authority granted through Christ. By proclaiming the blood of Jesus, believers tap into the continuous power of His sacrifice, breaking barriers, changing circumstances, and experiencing the fullness of God's promises. Through consistent declarations, they align themselves with the victory of the cross, reinforcing their faith and walking in the power of His blood every day.

Chapter Eight:
The Effects Of Blood In Daily Life

"Every drop of blood of Jesus applied in our daily proclamation in our daily life as a proclamation has a tremendous positive effect on our physical body, emotional, and spiritual life."

(Monika Starova)

The blood of Jesus is a transformative force that impacts every facet of a believer's daily life, extending beyond spiritual warfare and physical healing to include divine protection, guidance, and breakthroughs in personal circumstances. This divine provision, established through Jesus' ultimate sacrifice, creates a protective shield against the challenges of life, offering blessings and peace to those who apply it faithfully and intentionally.

Throughout Scripture, the power of the blood is portrayed as essential for redemption, protection, and deliverance. From the Passover in Exodus, where the blood of a lamb safeguarded the

Israelites from the destroyer, to the ultimate sacrifice of Jesus Christ, the power of the blood is unmistakable. Galatians 3:13-14 affirms that Jesus became a curse for us so that we might receive blessings in every aspect of our lives – our relationships, work, health, and more. However, these blessings are not automatic; they must be activated through daily proclamation and faith. By speaking the word of God and declaring the power of Jesus' blood, believers can unlock the treasures of peace, prosperity, and protection that God has intended for them.

**

Jesus sprinkled his blood seven times on the way to his crucifixion. The first shedding of his blood was in the Garden of Gethsemane. He sweated drops of blood because of the agony he felt when he considered the suffering he was going to experience. He left the will of the Father to contemplate his own distress. In the Garden of Eden, Adam lost his ability to say no to sin. However, Jesus, the new Adam, redeemed us from sin when he said no to his own desire. Luke 22:41-44 says, "And He was withdrawn from them about a stone's throw, and He knelt down and prayed, saying, 'Father, if it is your will, take this cup away from me; nevertheless, not My will, but Yours, be done.' Then an angel appeared to Him from heaven, strengthening Him. And being in agony, He prayed more earnestly. Then His sweat became like great drops of blood falling down to the ground." Here was Jesus' first sprinkling of his blood to redeem us from sin. We received liberty and forgiveness in Christ from our iniquities and our transgressions. Transgressions are sins we commit consciously. Iniquities are the sins of our forefathers which are passed down through generational lines through our bloodline from Adam to our fathers and grandfathers of today. The Lord also took all these sins with him. He became our sin that we might be forgiven and become righteous in the eyes of the Holy God.

The second shedding of blood is when Jesus went to the house of Caiaphas, the high priest. According to Matthew 26:65-67, "Then the high priest tore his clothes, his beard and hit Jesus in his face. They spat on him and his blood was shed, saying, 'He has spoken blasphemy! What further need do we have of witnesses? Look, now you have heard His blasphemy! What do you think?' They answered and said, 'He is deserving of death.' Then they spit in His face and beat Him; and others struck Him with the palms of their hands, saying, 'Prophesy to us, Christ! Who is the one who struck You!'" This is a fulfillment of Isaiah's prophecy about the mistreatment of the Lord Jesus Christ. He did not resist through all of this mistreatment. He had compassion for his people because he is God, the pure lamb of God. He endured the humiliation and mistreatment with humbleness, without fighting against it. In Isaiah 50:6, "I gave My back to those who struck Me, And My cheeks to those who plucked out the beard; I did not hide My face from shame and spitting."

The third time that Jesus' blood was shed happened after he went before Pontius Pilate. The people and priests asked Pilate to crucify him, and called for Barabbas, who was a murderer and a thief, to be released. They condemned the Lord to death on the cross and commanded a Roman soldier to scourge him on his back many times (Matthew 27:26). What was the significance of the scourging? He redeemed our sickness with his body. He endured all the scourges so that we might be healed. Isaiah 53:5 says, "But he was wounded for our transgressions, he was bruised for our iniquities, the chastisement of our peace was upon Him, and with his stripes we are healed." Scourging and crucifixion were the cruelest forms of punishment at that time. Matthew 27:27-28 says, "Then he released Barabbas to them;

and when he had scourged Jesus, he delivered Him to be crucified. Then the soldiers of the governor took Jesus into the Praetorium and gathered the whole garrison around Him. And they stripped Him and put a scarlet robe on Him." It was in the Praetorium where they scourged Him badly. The blood was shed from his back. He redeemed our health, our well-being, from any sickness, from sin and every curse. The Lord made us whole against the curse and the bondage, and healed us physically. Jesus shared his broken body with his disciples during the last supper with them. When he broke the bread, he showed that his body was going to be broken for their healing. Whoever receives Jesus is healed, is made whole from any sickness and disease, and from any bondage or curse.

Our suffering today is nothing compared to the suffering of the Lord Jesus Christ. His flesh was torn as a result of being whipped 39 times. His face was disfigured. His head was crushed from being beaten repeatedly. He suffered rejection, mockery, and humiliation while he was nailed to the cross. He took our shame and humiliation so that we may share his glory. He was punished so that we might be forgiven. He was bruised that we might be healed. He became the curse that we might have the blessings. He was whipped 39 times. According to Jewish law, one may be whipped 40 times, but they always stopped at the 39th stroke because they believed the 40th stroke could be fatal for the person being whipped. The whip had nine strands. Each strand had balls, pieces of sharp nails, bones, and metal on it. He was so badly beaten that he was not recognizable as a human being.

The fourth shedding of the blood of Jesus occurred when they put the thorns on his head. Matthew 27:29-31 says, "When they had twisted a crown of thorns, they put it on His head, and a reed in His right hand. And they bowed their knees before Him and mocked Him, saying, 'Hail, King of the Jews!' Then they spat on Him, and took the reed and struck Him on the head. And when they had mocked Him, they took the robe off Him, put His own clothes on Him, and led Him away to be crucified." After putting the crown on his head, they pushed the thorns into his head towards his brain, and hit him on the head, so that blood ran down over his face. The crown of big, thick thorns was forced onto his head. The Lord suffered much from the crown on his head in order to heal our minds and release our thoughts from the forces of darkness and send us into the light. His blood freed our minds so the enemy had no control over our thoughts. The blood flowed from his head and redeemed our minds, giving us freedom from our mental torture. Isaiah 53:5 says, "But he was pierced for our transgressions, he was crushed for our iniquities; the punishment that brought us peace was on him, and by his wounds we are healed." We are free from the witchcraft that torments our minds. We are lost from any depression and suffering in our minds. We can make the right choices for our destiny in our minds because of the blood of Jesus.

Jesus' blood was shed a fifth time when they pierced his hands. David spoke of this in the Psalms, saying, "For dogs have surrounded Me; The congregation of the wicked has enclosed Me. They pierced My hands and my feet" (Psalm 22:16). David, through the Holy Spirit, prophesied about the suffering of Jesus, as David himself never experienced such torment. The piercing of the hands represents the redemption of all actions taken by humanity. It signifies cleansing from generational bondages and transgressions, offering holy hands to those who follow Christ. Through his suffering, the children of God are made clean, and their hands are no longer bound by sin. The work of their hands is now blessed, and they are free to create, build, and succeed for the glory of God. The curse upon human labor is lifted, and whatever is done in the name of Christ shall prosper.

The sixth shedding of blood occurred when they pierced his feet. The Psalms also foretell this suffering: "They pierced ... My feet" (Psalm 22:16). When Adam and Eve sinned, they lost the dominion that God had given them over the earth. Satan took authority over them because of their disobedience. Jesus, through his sacrifice, bought back this dominion with his blood. Dominion is represented in the feet, as it is by the feet that people walk in authority. Luke 10:19 states, "Behold, I give to you authority to tread on serpents and scorpions, and all over the authority of the enemy, and nothing shall by any means hurt you." Through the piercing of Jesus' feet, humanity is redeemed from the bondage of sin that restricts them from walking in God's will. Spiritual captivity is broken, and those who follow Christ are freed from the snares of darkness. By the sacrifice of Jesus, believers have power over evil, and their feet carry them to spread blessings rather than bondage. Their paths are made righteous, and they walk in the freedom of Christ, no longer weighed down by the chains of past generations.

The final shedding of Jesus' blood occurred when they pierced his side. "But one of the soldiers pierced His side with a spear, and immediately blood and water came out" (John 19:34). This moment carried deep significance, as both blood and water flowed. The blood symbolized complete redemption, while the water represented the baptism of the Holy Spirit. Jesus' suffering not only redeemed humanity from sin but also offered spiritual renewal. His sacrifice healed broken hearts, bringing joy and purpose where there was once pain. On the cross, Jesus felt the ultimate weight of rejection. He was abandoned by his Father in order to fulfill his mission, and even his disciples deserted him. Apart from John, none of those closest to him remained at his side. His agony was immense, both physically and emotionally. His heart was heavy with sorrow, having been betrayed by Judas and rejected by the very people he had come to save. When the soldier thrust the spear into his side, it was as if the pain of a broken heart was made physical.

God is the healer of the brokenhearted, and Jesus' suffering provided that healing for all who believe in him. During his ministry, Jesus declared that he had come to heal the brokenhearted, and through his death, he fulfilled this promise. His body was emptied of blood, poured out for the redemption of the world. His sacrifice was complete, given without reservation. Every drop of his blood speaks on behalf of those who believe in him, offering salvation, healing, and restoration.

The Old Testament repeatedly emphasizes the significance of blood. Leviticus 17 commands the Jewish people not to consume blood, stating in verse 11, "For the life of the flesh is in the blood, and I have given it to you upon the altar to make atonement for your souls." This was a foreshadowing of the ultimate sacrifice of Christ. Isaiah 53:12 further prophesies, "Therefore I will divide Him (Jesus) a portion with the great, And He shall divide the spoil with the strong, Because He poured out His soul (his life) unto death, And He was numbered with the transgressors, And He bore the sin of many, and made intercession for the transgressors." Isaiah's words described the crucifixion centuries before it happened, foretelling how Jesus would hang between two thieves and how his blood would cover the sins of all transgressors. Because of his sacrifice, Jesus now intercedes for humanity before the Father. His blood speaks, not just as a symbol, but as a living testimony of redemption.

The price of salvation was immense. Jesus gave everything he had, even being buried in a borrowed tomb. It cost him his very life to redeem the world. Now, it is the responsibility of all believers to apply the blood of Jesus to their lives, to believe in him, and to spread his message. Proclaiming his word is an essential part of this mission, ensuring that all people understand what Christ has done for the salvation of humanity. The blood of Jesus was shed to prepare believers for his return. When he comes again, those who have been redeemed will live with him eternally, free from death, sorrow, and fear. They will know only joy, happiness, and eternal life in his presence.

**

The blood of Jesus Christ is central to the Christian faith, and its power is manifested in seven foundational ways that radically transform the life of every believer. The first effect is justification. Through His blood, believers are declared righteous before God, as if they had never sinned. Romans 5:9 says, "Since we have now been justified by His blood, how much more shall we be saved from God's wrath through Him?" This means we stand blameless in God's sight, not because of our works but because of Christ's sacrifice. The second effect is life. Jesus said in John 6:53, "Unless you eat the flesh of the Son of Man and drink His blood, you have no life in you." His blood imparts divine life to our spirit, energizing our souls with His eternal presence.

The third effect is the forgiveness of sin. Ephesians 1:7 declares, "In Him we have redemption through His blood, the forgiveness of sins." The blood doesn't just cover our sins; it removes them completely, giving us a clean slate before God. The fourth is access to God's throne. Hebrews 10:19 proclaims that "we have confidence to enter the Most Holy Place by the blood of Jesus." No longer distant from God, we can now come boldly before Him with our prayers and needs. The fifth is breaking bondage. Revelation 1:5 tells us that Jesus "has freed us from our sins by His blood." Every chain of addiction, oppression, or generational curse can be broken through the blood.

The sixth effect is sanctification – being set apart for God. Hebrews 13:12 says, "Jesus also suffered...to sanctify the people through His own blood." The blood not only saves us but also purifies our lives, making us holy vessels for God's purposes. Finally, the seventh effect is eternal life. Through His blood, we are promised an inheritance that never fades. Revelation 7:14 describes those who "have washed their robes and made them white in the blood of the Lamb." These effects are not just theological ideas but powerful truths that work in the life of every believer. Each benefit must be believed, received, and declared with faith.

**

In daily life, the blood of Jesus provides divine protection in ways that often defy natural understanding. The testimony of the Israelites during the Passover is a vivid example. God commanded each household to apply the blood of a lamb to their doorframes, assuring them that when the destroyer passed through the land, those homes marked by the blood would be spared. This is proven by Exodus 12:13-28 (NIV), which states, "The blood will be a sign for you on the houses where you are, and when I see the blood, I will pass over you. No destructive plague will touch you when I strike Egypt..." This act of faith and obedience became a symbol of divine protection, prefiguring the protective power of Jesus' blood. As 1 Corinthians 5:7 states, "Christ, our Passover lamb, has been sacrificed." His blood now serves as the ultimate source of protection, shielding believers from harm, curses, and spiritual attacks when proclaimed over their lives.

The protective power of the blood is not limited to ancient times. Modern testimonies of divine intervention serve as powerful reminders of its continued effectiveness. One such account comes from a time of civil unrest in Albania during the late 1990s. Amid a violent civil war, criminal gangs roamed the streets, looting and targeting homes. My family became a potential target due to my father's role in safeguarding national treasures. In the face of imminent danger, I turned to faith, praying Psalm 23 and proclaiming the blood of Jesus over my home. My faith-filled declarations brought protection; the gang that was set to attack our house moved on to another, leaving us unharmed. This testimony illustrates that the blood of Jesus, when applied through prayer and proclamation, acts as a tangible barrier against danger.

The blood also has the power to bring breakthroughs in personal circumstances. It is not uncommon for believers to encounter situations where they feel helpless, whether in finances, relationships, or health. In such moments, the blood of Jesus becomes a powerful tool for intercession. By approaching the throne of grace with faith and humility, believers can plead the blood of Jesus over their situations, inviting divine intervention and favor. For instance, in cases of financial struggles, believers can pray and proclaim the blood over their resources, asking God to remove any hindrance or attack from the enemy and to release His blessings. This act of faith aligns with God's promises and activates His provision in ways that often seem miraculous.

The story of a doctor who faced challenges with his business highlights how the blood of Jesus can work in seemingly insurmountable situations. His clinic was removed from Google's advertising platform due to a compliance issue, severely impacting his ability to reach patients. Feeling desperate, he turned to prayer, applying the principles of proclaiming the blood of Jesus and presenting his case before the heavenly courts. Within 48 hours, the issue was resolved, and his clinic's advertisements were restored. This example demonstrates that the blood of Jesus, combined with faith and proclamation, can bring resolution and favor in the most unexpected ways.

The daily application of the blood of Jesus is a practical and powerful practice that equips believers to navigate life's challenges. Just as the Israelites had to actively apply the blood of the Passover lamb to their doorframes, believers today must intentionally declare and apply the blood over every area of their lives. In Exodus 12, God commanded the Israelites to take the blood of a spotless lamb and apply it to the doorposts and lintels of their homes as a sign of protection against the final plague in Egypt – the death of the firstborn. Exodus 12:13 (NIV) states, "The blood will be a sign for you on the houses where you are, and when I see the blood, I will pass over you. No destructive plague will touch you when I strike Egypt." This act of obedience ensured that the Israelites were spared from judgment, demonstrating the power of sacrificial blood as a covering of protection and deliverance.

God told Moses that the father of each house should take a lamb without blemish, slaughter it, and apply its blood to the doorframes using hyssop branches. This act of obedience ensured divine protection. It was crucial that the blood was not just collected but actively applied. Families that followed this command were shielded from destruction, reinforcing that obedience is necessary for divine covering. The hyssop branch used to apply the blood symbolizes the Word of God, which believers must use to apply the promises of Christ's blood in their lives today.

The significance of the Passover blood extends beyond Israel's physical deliverance from Egypt; it foreshadowed the ultimate redemption found in Jesus Christ. Just as the lamb's blood saved the

Israelites from destruction, the blood of Jesus saves believers from sin and eternal separation from God. 1 Corinthians 5:7 explicitly states, "Christ, our Passover lamb, has been sacrificed." His blood removes sin completely, unlike the Old Testament sacrificial system, which required repeated atonement. Hebrews 9:26 affirms that Jesus has "removed sin by sacrificing Himself." The Old Testament practice of annual sacrifices only covered sin temporarily, but Christ's sacrifice was perfect and complete, securing eternal redemption.

God instituted the Passover as a lasting ordinance, instructing the Israelites to observe it throughout the generations. It was not merely a ritual but a covenantal act, symbolizing God's promise of protection and deliverance. In the same way, Jesus' blood represents the new covenant, reconciling believers to God and granting eternal life. The Apostle Peter echoes this in 1 Peter 1:2, stating that believers must be "obedient to Jesus Christ and sprinkled with His blood." Just as the Israelites had to obey and remain inside their homes for the blood to be effective, faith and obedience are necessary to fully experience the power of Jesus' blood today.

The blood of Jesus not only provides salvation but also grants victory over death and the enemy. 1 Corinthians 15:55-57 declares, "O death, where is your victory? O death, where is your sting? Thanks be to God! He gives us the victory through our Lord Jesus Christ." Sin entered humanity through Adam, and its consequence is death. However, Jesus' sacrifice broke this curse, giving believers the hope of eternal life. His blood has opened the gates of salvation, securing triumph over sin, hell, and death itself.

Jesus, as both the High Priest and the sacrificial offering, fulfilled the ultimate atonement. Hebrews 9:13-14 states, "If the blood of goats and bulls sanctifies for the purifying of the flesh, how much more shall the blood of Christ, who through the eternal Spirit offered Himself without blemish to God, cleanse your conscience from dead works to serve the living God?" His sacrifice was perfect and final, removing the need for continual offerings. The Old Testament Day of Atonement (Yom Kippur) was an annual reminder of sin, whereas Christ's atonement permanently removes sin for those who believe.

The power of the blood is activated through faith, obedience, and alignment with God's will. Jesus' entire ministry was empowered by the Holy Spirit, enabling Him to perform miracles and bring deliverance (Luke 4:18). As believers apply His blood through faith, they step into divine protection, provision, and victory. Jesus himself declared in John 15:7, "If you abide in me and my words abide in you, ask whatever you desire, and it shall be done for you." This underscores the necessity of not only trusting in His blood but also abiding in His Word and Spirit.

Moreover, the blood of Jesus offers divine guidance in decision-making. Life is filled with moments of uncertainty, where the right path is not always clear. By pleading the blood over their choices, believers invite the wisdom and direction of the Holy Spirit. The blood serves as a spiritual compass, guiding them away from harm and toward God's perfect plan for their lives. This guidance often manifests in peace, clarity, and an inner assurance that surpasses human understanding.

In relationships, the blood of Jesus works to bring healing, unity, and reconciliation. Many families and friendships are plagued by division, misunderstandings, and pain. By declaring the blood over these relationships, believers can break the chains of bitterness and unforgiveness, inviting God's restorative power to work in their hearts and the hearts of others. The blood of Jesus reminds us of the ultimate reconciliation achieved on the cross, where humanity was restored to a right relationship with God. This same power can mend even the most fractured relationships, bringing peace and harmony.

Faith plays a crucial role in experiencing the effects of the blood in daily life. Hebrews 11:6 reminds us that "without faith, it is impossible to please God." Faith transforms declarations into spiritual realities, bridging the gap between God's promises and the believer's circumstances. It is not enough to simply know about the power of the blood; believers must actively apply it with unwavering faith, trusting in its ability to protect, heal, and provide.

The blood of Jesus also serves as a safeguard against the spiritual forces of jealousy, envy, and the evil eye. These forces often operate subtly, causing disruption and harm in people's lives. By proclaiming the blood over themselves and their loved ones, believers create a spiritual shield that renders these attacks ineffective. The blood of Jesus is a reminder to the enemy that his power has been defeated, and he cannot harm those who are covered by it.

The effects of the blood extend to every aspect of life, from work and finances to health and relationships. Its power is not confined to moments of crisis but is available for daily application, transforming ordinary situations into opportunities for God's glory to be revealed. Believers who make the blood a central part of their spiritual practice experience a profound sense of peace, knowing that they are protected, guided, and empowered by the ultimate sacrifice of Jesus Christ. This peace, rooted in the blood, enables them to face life's challenges with confidence and hope.

The significance of the blood does not end with Christ's crucifixion – it carries into eternity, as seen in Revelation 5:9, which states: *"And they sang a new song, saying: 'You are worthy to take the scroll and to open its seals, because you were slain, and with your blood you purchased for God persons from every tribe and language and people and nation.'"* This verse highlights the universal power of Christ's blood, demonstrating that His sacrifice was not limited to one group but extended to all humanity. The blood of Jesus has redeemed people from every nation, bringing them into the kingdom of God. This global redemption underscores the boundless reach of the blood's power – not only in granting eternal salvation but also in shaping the daily lives of believers. It serves as a continual source of protection, guidance, and transformation, reminding believers that they belong to a kingdom where Christ reigns as the victorious Lamb.

The daily application of the blood of Jesus has transformative potential, impacting work, relationships, and decision-making in practical and profound ways. When believers intentionally live a life covered by the blood, they open themselves to divine intervention, peace, and prosperity in the most ordinary aspects of existence. This active reliance on the power of the blood reshapes their experiences and reveals God's faithfulness in daily life.

Incorporating the blood of Jesus into one's spiritual routine strengthens faith and creates a spiritual foundation for facing life's challenges. The habit of proclaiming the blood in daily prayers can become a routine that not only uplifts but also empowers believers to overcome difficulties. Whether during moments of gratitude, need, or adversity, invoking the blood reminds believers of their spiritual identity and the victory they have in Christ. By declaring, "The blood of Jesus covers my home, family, and work," believers acknowledge their reliance on divine grace while inviting God's presence into every part of their lives.

The blood of Jesus has ten profound effects in a believer's life, shaping their spiritual journey and daily experiences. First, it brings redemption (Revelation 5:9), purchasing believers from sin and the power of the enemy. Second, it provides cleansing (1 John 1:7), continuously purifying hearts and removing the guilt of sin. Third, the blood justifies (Romans 5:9), making believers righteous before God as if they had never sinned. Fourth, it sanctifies (Hebrews 13:12), setting them apart for God's purposes and making them holy. Fifth, the blood grants salvation (Romans 10:9), securing eternal life for those who accept Christ. Sixth, it gives access to God's presence and intercession (Hebrews 4:16), allowing believers to boldly approach the throne of grace. Seventh, the blood brings divine protection (Exodus 12:13), shielding them from harm and spiritual attacks. Eighth, it empowers believers to overcome the enemy (Revelation 12:11), breaking strongholds and ensuring victory over darkness. Ninth, the blood provides healing (Isaiah 53:5), restoring physical, emotional, and spiritual well-being. Finally, it establishes peace and reconciliation (Colossians 1:20), mending broken relationships and uniting believers with God.

The practical application of the blood of Jesus becomes particularly evident in the workplace, where believers often encounter challenges such as stress, competition, and difficult relationships. Praying and proclaiming the blood over one's work environment fosters a sense of divine protection and guidance. This practice can help to create an atmosphere of peace, clarity, and integrity. For example, before beginning a project, a believer might pray, "Lord, I plead the blood of Jesus over this task. Guide my efforts, bless the work of my hands, and grant me favor." Such prayers not only invite divine assistance but also encourage a mindset of reliance on God's provision.

In relationships, the blood of Jesus brings restoration and fosters unity. Many conflicts arise from misunderstandings, unmet expectations, or spiritual attacks that seek to divide families, friends, and communities. Declaring the blood of Jesus over these relationships helps to break chains of discord and promotes reconciliation. When believers proclaim the blood over their loved ones, they invoke God's peace and protection, creating an environment where love and forgiveness can flourish. This practice extends to difficult relationships as well, where the power of the blood can soften hearts and pave the way for healing.

The transformative effects of the blood are also evident in decision-making, where it provides clarity and protection against confusion. Life often requires navigating complex choices, and fear of making the wrong decision can lead to anxiety. Pleading the blood of Jesus over these decisions invites the Holy Spirit's guidance, ensuring alignment with God's will. For example, a believer facing a significant career choice might pray, "I plead the blood of Jesus over this decision, asking for wisdom and discernment. Guide me, Lord, and close any door that is not from You." This act of faith opens the door to divine direction, allowing the believer to proceed with confidence and peace.

The blood of Jesus not only transforms internal attitudes but also has the power to bring peace and prosperity to external circumstances. The peace that comes from living a life covered by blood surpasses human understanding, as promised in Philippians 4:7. This peace is not merely the absence of conflict but a deep sense of assurance that God is in control. By declaring the blood over their homes, believers can create sanctuaries of peace, shielding their households from spiritual attacks and fostering an atmosphere of love and joy. This peace extends into all areas of life, enabling believers to navigate trials with calm and trust.

The prosperity associated with the blood of Jesus goes beyond financial blessings, encompassing holistic well-being and the fulfillment of God's promises. When believers apply the blood to their lives, they align themselves with the abundant life that Jesus promised in John 10:10. This alignment often manifests in breakthroughs, favor, and unexpected blessings. For instance, someone struggling in their career might experience a sudden opportunity or promotion after committing their work to God and proclaiming the blood of Jesus over their efforts. Such experiences testify to the blood's ability to unlock divine provision and demonstrate God's faithfulness.

The practical aspects of living a life covered by blood are not limited to grand gestures or dramatic events. They are evident in the small, consistent actions that reflect a heart surrendered to God. By cultivating a habit of daily proclamations, believers ensure that they remain connected to the source of their strength and protection. This routine might include prayers such as, "By the blood of Jesus, I declare that I am free from fear and anxiety," or "I plead the blood of Jesus over my family, asking for protection, unity, and blessings." These declarations not only reinforce faith but also create a spiritual atmosphere where God's presence is actively invited.

The blood of Jesus has the power to transform ordinary situations into extraordinary testimonies of God's grace. By applying the blood to their lives, believers can experience a breakthrough in areas where they previously faced obstacles. For example, someone struggling with a strained family relationship might begin to see reconciliation after committing the matter to God and proclaiming the blood over the situation. Similarly, a believer experiencing financial difficulties might witness unexpected provisions after faithfully applying the blood in their prayers. These transformations serve as reminders that God's power is not confined to spiritual matters but extends into every corner of daily life.

The ultimate effect of the blood in daily life is the tangible evidence of God's love and power. Through faith-filled proclamations and consistent application, believers can experience a life marked by peace, protection, and prosperity. This way of living is not limited to moments of crisis but becomes a continual expression of reliance on God. The blood of Jesus, shed once for all, remains a source of strength and hope for those who choose to walk in its power, transforming every aspect of their lives into a reflection of God's glory and goodness.

Chapter Nine:
Breaking Curses And Strongholds Through Blood

"There is an amazing power in the perfect sacrifice of the blood of Jesus. Every communion we take daily releases us from the power of the darkness of this world."

(Monika Starova)

The blood of Jesus stands as the most powerful tool for breaking curses and demolishing strongholds that keep people bound in spiritual oppression. Many individuals, though physically free, live in spiritual bondage, trapped in cycles of failure, addiction, and oppression. These unseen chains prevent them from walking in the fullness of God's blessings and hinder their purpose. However, through the blood of Jesus, all curses – whether generational, self-imposed, or placed by others – can be broken. The authority that Christ has given believers through His sacrifice enables them to overcome spiritual attacks, destroy demonic influences, and live in freedom.

Curses have been recognized in the Bible as real spiritual forces that impact people's lives. They manifest in different ways, including sickness, financial struggles, repeated failures, and destructive patterns passed down through generations. In Galatians 3:13-14, the Bible states that "Christ redeemed us from the curse of the law by becoming a curse for us, for it is written: 'Cursed is everyone who is hung on a pole.' He redeemed us so that the blessing given to Abraham might come to the Gentiles through Christ Jesus, so that by faith we might receive the promise of the Spirit." This passage reveals that Jesus bore every curse on the cross, making a way for believers to walk in the blessings of God. However, breaking free from these curses requires faith, persistence, and the application of the blood of Jesus.

One of the most common forms of spiritual bondage is generational curses – patterns of misfortune, sin, or sickness that seem to follow families from one generation to the next. Many people struggle with the same problems their parents or grandparents faced, whether it be poverty, broken marriages, chronic illness, or addictions. The root of these issues is often spiritual, requiring a spiritual solution. Exodus 20:5 speaks of God visiting "the iniquity of the fathers on the children to the third and fourth generation of those who hate me." However, through the blood of Jesus, these generational patterns can be broken. When a believer declares, "The blood of Jesus sets me free from every generational curse," they are enforcing the victory of Christ in their lives. They are rejecting the enemy's claim and standing under the covenant of Christ's blood, which speaks a better word than the curses of the past.

Many people unknowingly live under spiritual strongholds that keep them from achieving their goals and fulfilling their divine purpose. They move from job to job, relationship to relationship, always searching but never finding satisfaction. They face unseen barriers that block their progress, making life feel like a constant battle. This was a reality for many, including me, who once lived in a cycle of unfinished projects, unwise decisions, and rebellion against God's direction. Without seeking God's counsel, they pursued their own path, only to encounter frustration and failure. However, God's mercy is always available to those who return to Him with a repentant heart. Through repentance, the application of the blood of Jesus, and alignment with God's will, these cycles of delay and failure can be broken.

In addition to generational curses and strongholds of failure, many people are bound by addictions and destructive habits. Bondage to substances such as alcohol, cigarettes, or even seemingly harmless habits like overeating, oversleeping, and gossiping can be spiritual chains that keep individuals enslaved. The Bible warns against these things, as they open doors for the enemy to gain influence. Sexual sins, including pornography, masturbation, and immoral thoughts, are also powerful strongholds that entangle people and separate them from God's presence. John 8:34 states, "Very truly I tell you, everyone who sins is a slave to sin." However, the good news is found in John 8:36: "So if the Son sets you free, you will be free indeed." True freedom comes through Christ alone, and His blood is the key to breaking every chain of addiction.

Strongholds operate in the mind, influencing thoughts and decisions. They create patterns of negative thinking that make it difficult for individuals to break free from sin. The Bible teaches in 2 Corinthians 10:3-5 that believers must actively fight against these strongholds: "For though we walk in the flesh, we do not war according to the flesh. For the weapons of our warfare are not carnal but mighty in God for pulling down strongholds, casting down arguments and every high thing that exalts itself against the knowledge of God, bringing every thought into captivity to the obedience of Christ." The blood of Jesus cleanses not only the body but also the mind, breaking the power of negative thought patterns and replacing them with the truth of God's Word. By constantly proclaiming the power of the blood, believers renew their minds and reject the lies of the enemy.

One of the most dangerous forms of spiritual oppression comes from witchcraft, sorcery, and demonic attacks. Many people suffer from unexplained misfortunes, sicknesses, or disturbances in their homes without realizing they may be under spiritual attack. Curses, spells, and occult practices are real, and their effects can bring destruction into people's lives. However, the blood of Jesus has supreme authority over every power of darkness. Revelation 12:11 declares, "They triumphed over him by the blood of the Lamb and by the word of their testimony." This means that believers have the power to overcome any demonic influence through the blood of Jesus and their spoken declarations.

Jesus has given His followers the authority to cast out demons and break the chains of darkness. Luke 10:19 states, "Behold, I give you authority to tread over serpents and scorpions, and over all the power of the enemy, and nothing shall in any way hurt you." This authority is rooted in a close relationship with Christ. Demons recognize authority and respond to those who walk in the power of Jesus' name. In Acts 19:13-16, the sons of Sceva attempted to cast out demons in Jesus' name, but because they had no true relationship with Him, the demons overpowered them. This serves as a reminder that believers must be spiritually prepared, covered by the blood of Jesus, and walk in righteousness to exercise power over darkness.

Persistent prayer and proclamation play a crucial role in breaking curses and strongholds. The enemy does not give up easily, and breaking free from spiritual oppression requires consistency. Believers must continually declare the blood of Jesus over their lives, homes, families, and work. Declaring, "I plead the blood of Jesus over my mind, my body, and my spirit," is a powerful act of faith that establishes God's protection and destroys the enemy's plans. Every day, believers should pray, covering themselves in the blood of Jesus and standing on the promises of God's Word. Additionally, taking communion daily is a spiritual act of breaking free from darkness.

Discernment is also essential in identifying spiritual attacks and responding effectively. Many people experience recurring dreams, unexplained fear, or persistent obstacles that indicate the presence of spiritual warfare. Instead of ignoring these signs, believers should seek God in prayer and ask for wisdom. Through the blood of Jesus and the authority of His name, every attack of the enemy can be neutralized.

Throughout the Bible, from Genesis to Revelation, the significance of the blood as a means of purification, cleansing, and victory is undeniable. The blood of Jesus is not just a theological concept; it is a living, powerful force that protects, redeems, and delivers those who apply it in faith. I have personally experienced its power, and I want to share with you how the blood of Jesus broke the strongholds and generational curses that once ruled my life and family.

I was born into a Muslim family where witchcraft, jealousy, and curses were an unfortunate reality. My grandmother was deeply involved in occult practices, and her hatred toward my mother was so strong that she cursed her during pregnancy. She declared that my mother would not give birth to children but to serpents instead. Despite this curse, my twin brother and I were born. However, while he was delivered normally, I came into the world nearly lifeless, my body completely blue, struggling between life and death. It was as if the enemy had a plan to take me before I could even draw my first breath. But when the enemy plots destruction, God always has a greater plan. The Lord intervened, using a nurse who instinctively turned me upside down and revived me. My mother, however, lost an unusual amount of blood and was diagnosed with heart complications. I believe that Satan wanted to use that moment as a blood sacrifice, but the blood of Jesus overruled it. The Lord had destined me to live, and His hand was upon my life even from birth.

On January 1, 2009, during the early morning hours, I saw Christ in my dream. I saw all that He suffered on the cross, and it was like a vision. I had never felt so much emotion in my life. I woke at 3 a.m. from the overwhelming intensity of it. The wounds I saw in the dream, the torment He endured, left an imprint on my soul. In the vision, I was outside Jerusalem, at Golgotha, where He was crucified. Golgotha, 'Kraniou Topos' in Greek, means the place of the skull. There, I saw Christ carrying the cross, His body weak from the lashes, His face unrecognizable beneath the blood that streamed down. The Roman officers pushed Him forward, and the people jeered. The street was stained with His blood where He had fallen.

As I walked with Him, I witnessed the cruelty, the rejection, and the mockery. The man who helped carry His cross was struggling, yet Jesus continued without complaint. Though He was God, He bore this suffering willingly, fulfilling what was written in Isaiah 53:12: "And he was numbered with the transgressors, and he bore the sins of many, and made intercession for the transgressors." Under the cross, I felt the weight of His sacrifice. His blood fell upon me, and in that moment, I understood the depth of His suffering. The pain I felt in my soul was but a fraction of what He endured for all of us.

I saw them binding His feet and hands with a thick rope. They offered Him sour vinegar, the drink meant to numb the condemned, but He refused. He chose to bear the pain in full. He took upon Himself all iniquity, all sin, all filthiness. I wept as I watched the people who had once praised Him now turn against Him. Darkness filled the sky, the clouds thick and heavy. Thunder roared. The wind howled. And then He spoke to me.

"Take up your cross, bear my yoke," He said. "My yoke is easy, my burden is light. Announce my name to the world. Many are oppressed, possessed, and living in bondage. Declare my blood to the people. My blood is powerful enough to give them eternal life. Humanity cannot buy salvation with money, pride, or power. But my blood washes away all sin. The world was lost through Adam, but I have come as the second Adam to restore life."

Then I heard Him say, "It is finished."

When I woke at 3 a.m. on the first day of 2010, my heart was heavy with the revelation. I immediately shared what I had seen with a friend. The love of Christ is beyond human comprehension. God's love is so immense that He sacrificed His Son for us. When Jesus declared, "It is finished," He meant that the perfect atonement was complete. His ministry, from beginning to end, was flawless. As Derek Prince once said, Jesus began His ministry perfectly and finished it perfectly. Pastor Benny Hinn speaks of the atonement before the cross as the salvation of our souls and the atonement behind the cross as the healing we receive. As Isaiah 53:5 says, "By His stripes, we are healed."

WHY THE SHEDDING OF THE BLOOD?

In Leviticus, atonement is mentioned 51 times, meaning "to cover" or "to make a covering." Leviticus 17:11 states, "For the life of the flesh is in the blood, and I have given it to you upon the altar to make atonement for your souls; for it is the blood that makes atonement for the soul." This truth carries into the New Testament, as Hebrews 9:22 affirms, "Without the shedding of blood, there is no forgiveness."

Our blood carries oxygen, the body's most vital nutrient. A body can survive with failing organs, but the heart's failure means inevitable death. That is why atonement is through blood. The Old Testament sacrifices, repeated daily, foreshadowed the ultimate sacrifice of Christ. Jesus, fully God and fully man, was the pure offering, the everlasting atonement for sin. Hebrews 8-10 confirms this. His blood not only secures eternal life but also heals our hearts, minds, bodies, and souls.

I have learned from my own life experiences, mistakes, and sins that there is power in the blood. No force of darkness, no witchcraft, no evil spirit can prevail when we apply the blood of Jesus and declare His word. The Bible does not go into detail about the extent of Christ's physical suffering, but what I saw in my vision was beyond human endurance. The beatings, the mockery, the nails driven through His flesh – He bore it all for us. He carried our shame, guilt, sickness, and poverty so that we might receive joy, peace, healing, and abundance. His blood still speaks today, as powerfully as it did on the day of His crucifixion.

I cover myself with His blood daily. When I pray, I speak protection over my life, my family, my home, my work, and my church. I declare: "I cover myself, my family, my job, my finances, my mind, my soul, and every distraction of this life with the precious blood of Jesus. I cover my house, my children, and my friends. I declare protection over my life from the crown of my head to the soles of my feet." This blood, shed over two thousand years ago, has never lost its power.

The cross was not the end. Jesus rose, victorious, and so we are victorious in Him. We are no longer children of the first Adam who fell, but of the second Adam, Christ, who overcame. As 1 John 3:2 says, "Beloved, now we are children of God, and it has not yet been revealed what we shall be, but we know that when He is revealed, we shall be like Him, for we shall see Him as He is." Though we are in this world, we are also partakers of His divine nature. One day, we will see Him as He is, and we will be transformed fully into His likeness.

Genesis 1:27 tells us we were made in His image. The enemy seeks to distort this truth, to burden us with doubt, fear, and guilt. But the blood of Jesus has freed us. We are victorious. We are redeemed. We are covered by His sacrifice. No evil can stand against the power of His blood. I am thankful each day that I can take communion, receiving the bread as His flesh and the wine as His blood, remembering the covenant He established.

From the day I was born, my grandmother saw me as an enemy because her wicked plans had failed. She spent her days speaking spells and curses over my family, creating an atmosphere of fear, conflict, and oppression in our home. Arguments, tension, and spiritual heaviness filled our lives daily. It wasn't until I turned eleven that the darkness began to lift – my grandmother passed away, and suddenly, peace entered our home. For the first time, we could live without fear. It was at this age that I first heard about Jesus Christ through American missionaries who came to Albania. Their message of salvation stirred something in me, and I accepted Christ into my heart. Although I was still living in a Muslim household, I began to feel the presence of God in my life. The more I learned about Christ, the more I realized that the darkness I had lived under was not normal – it was the result of generational curses and occult involvement that had plagued my family for years.

In my culture, covenants sealed by blood have been a significant part of tradition. One of the most well-known is called **Besa**, a pledge of honor that must be kept in secrecy and loyalty. As a child, I made a blood covenant with a friend, sealing our bond by cutting our thumbs and mixing our blood. In that moment, we vowed to defend each other until death. I later realized that this was not just an innocent childhood act – it was a spiritual covenant that had unseen consequences. Blood covenants are deeply rooted in many cultures, and they create strongholds that keep people bound unless they are broken by the blood of Jesus.

A more dangerous blood covenant in my family was one of vengeance, known as **Gjakmarrja**, or "blood-taking." This was a legal form of revenge in my culture, where if a person was murdered, their family had the right to kill in return. My grandfather was caught in this cycle of vengeance. He had a **Besa** agreement with his father-in-law regarding property and inheritance, but when his father-in-law broke the agreement, my grandfather killed him in front of the entire family. Years later, his brother-in-law avenged the murder by ambushing and killing my grandfather on his way home. My grandmother, who had already suffered the trauma of losing her father, now became a widow with two small children, one of whom was my father. The bloodshed brought immense pain, and bitterness filled my grandmother's heart, driving her deeper into occult practices. She cursed our family daily, binding us with spiritual chains that affected every generation that followed.

I grew up witnessing the effects of these blood covenants firsthand. The generational curses led to endless family conflicts, failures, and strife. It was only after coming to Christ that I understood why these patterns persisted. Satan uses bloodshed and covenants to keep people in bondage, fueling cycles of destruction within families. But the blood of Jesus is more powerful than any blood covenant made by man. As I grew in my faith, I began to renounce these curses and proclaim the blood of Jesus over my family. The transformation was undeniable. The strongholds that had kept my family in conflict and bitterness began to break. I forgave my grandmother, even though she had long passed away. The weight of generational sin was lifted, and peace replaced the turmoil that had defined our lives for decades.

Through my own journey, I have seen that nothing–not ancestral curses, not witchcraft, not even covenants sealed in blood–can stand against the power of Jesus' sacrifice. Hebrews 12:24 says we have come "to Jesus the mediator of the new covenant, and to the sprinkled blood that speaks a better word than the blood of Abel there." His blood speaks a better word, breaking the chains of the past and setting the captives free. The blood of Abel, as recorded in Genesis 4:10–11, cried out from the ground for vengeance after Cain murdered his brother. Abel's blood was shed unwillingly, a testimony of injustice and judgment. But the blood of Jesus, shed willingly, cries out for mercy and forgiveness. His sacrifice is the antidote to sin, overcoming judgment with grace. I stand here today as a living testimony that the blood of Jesus delivers, restores, and redeems. No matter what spiritual battles you face, no matter what curses or strongholds may be in your family, the blood of Jesus is the key to breaking every chain. By applying it with faith and proclaiming its power, you can walk in the freedom that Christ has already won for you.

The blood of Jesus is the ultimate weapon against every curse, stronghold, and demonic attack. It is not only a source of redemption but also a tool for deliverance. Those who apply it with faith experience freedom, breakthrough, and victory. Whether facing generational curses, personal struggles, addictions, or spiritual oppression, the answer is found in the blood of Jesus. By living a life surrendered to God, proclaiming His Word, and covering themselves in the blood, believers can walk in total freedom, breaking every chain and stepping into the abundant life that God has promised.

Chapter Ten:
Ten Effects Of The Blood Of Jesus

"The blood of Jesus frees and redeems us from the bondage of the devil and the evil powers of this world."

(Monika Starova)

The blood of Jesus is the most powerful force in existence, and its effects extend far beyond mere forgiveness of sins. It is also the ultimate force against demonic threats. While many Christians recognize the role of Jesus' blood in salvation, few fully understand the depth of its transformative power in daily life. The Bible reveals that the blood of Christ brings redemption, cleansing, justification, sanctification, and salvation, among other blessings. Each effect is essential to the believer's spiritual journey and offers a pathway to victory and communion with God.

From Genesis to Revelation, the significance of blood is evident. In the Old Testament, animal sacrifices temporarily atoned for sins, foreshadowing the ultimate sacrifice of Jesus Christ. The blood of lambs, bulls, and goats served as a temporary covering, but it was never enough to fully remove the stain of sin. Hebrews 9:12 states, "He entered once for all into the holy places, not by means of the blood of goats and calves but by means of his own blood, thus securing an eternal redemption." The sacrifice of Jesus was final, perfect, and sufficient for all time.

By understanding the ten key effects of the blood of Jesus, believers can apply its power in every aspect of their lives. This chapter will explore these effects, focusing on the ten foundational ones: redemption, cleansing, justification, sanctification, salvation, victory, protection, healing, access to God, and authority over the enemy. These are the cornerstones of a victorious Christian life.

1. Redemption Through the Blood

The first and most fundamental effect of the blood of Jesus is redemption. To redeem means to buy back or to pay the price for someone's freedom. The Greek word *agorazo*, used in Revelation 5:9, means "to purchase." Jesus' blood was the price paid to purchase humanity from the bondage of sin and the grip of the enemy. "For you were slain, and have redeemed us to God by your blood out of every tribe and tongue and people and nation" (Revelation 5:9).

Before Christ's sacrifice, humanity was enslaved to sin. The fall of Adam and Eve brought sin into the world, severing mankind's relationship with God. Every descendant of Adam inherited a fallen nature, bound by sin's dominion and subject to death. The Old Testament law highlighted the weight of sin but provided only a temporary covering through animal sacrifices. Hebrews 10:4 states, "For it is not possible that the blood of bulls and goats should take away sins." These sacrifices served as a foreshadowing of the perfect and ultimate sacrifice of Jesus, who redeemed humanity permanently.

Galatians 3:13 declares, "Christ has redeemed us from the curse of the law, having become a curse for us." This redemption is not just a theological concept; it has practical implications. The believer is no longer a slave to sin, fear, or condemnation. They are free to live in the fullness of God's blessings. Through His blood, Jesus rescued us from the kingdom of darkness and transferred us into His kingdom of light (Colossians 1:13-14).

Redemption is not merely about release from bondage – it is a legal transfer of ownership. Before salvation, every person belongs to the dominion of darkness, under the authority of Satan. But through the blood of Christ, believers are legally transferred into the kingdom of God. This transaction is not arbitrary; it fulfills the righteous justice of God, ensuring that sin's debt is fully paid. Isaiah 53:5 declares, "But He was wounded for our transgressions, He was bruised for our iniquities; The chastisement for our peace was upon Him, And by His stripes we are healed."

Furthermore, this redemption establishes a new covenant between God and His people. Under the old covenant, animal sacrifices were required for atonement, but Jesus, as the perfect Lamb of God, became the eternal sacrifice, fulfilling and surpassing the old system. Hebrews 9:15 states, "For this reason Christ is the mediator of a new covenant, that those who are called may receive the promised eternal inheritance – now that He has died as a ransom to set them free from the sins committed under the first covenant."

Redemption also applies to every area of life. Many believers struggle with cycles of failure, oppression, or bondage because they have not fully grasped their redemption in Christ. When a person is redeemed, they are no longer under the dominion of sin, sickness, poverty, or spiritual oppression. They are set free to live in the abundance of God's promises.

This redemption is activated through faith and proclamation. Psalm 107:2 instructs, "Let the redeemed of the Lord say so." The blood of Jesus is powerful, but believers must confess it over their lives. By daily declaring, "I am redeemed by the blood of Jesus from the hand of the enemy," they reinforce their spiritual position and prevent the enemy from regaining a foothold. Declaring redemption through the blood aligns a believer with God's will and releases them from every bondage the enemy tries to impose.

2. Cleansing and Forgiveness of Sins

The second effect of the blood of Jesus is cleansing. The blood does not merely cover sins as animal sacrifices did in the Old Testament – it washes them away completely. 1 John 1:7 proclaims, "But if we walk in the light, as he is in the light, we have fellowship with one another, and the blood of Jesus his Son cleanses us from all sin."

Sin defiles and separates a person from God, but the blood restores purity. The Greek word for cleansing, *katharizo*, means to purge and make free from contamination. This means that no matter how deep the stain of sin, the blood of Jesus has the power to purify completely. Isaiah 1:18 affirms this: "Though your sins are like scarlet, they shall be as white as snow." The imagery of being washed white as snow conveys the totality of God's forgiveness – sin is completely removed, leaving no trace of guilt or shame.

However, beyond mere forgiveness, the blood of Jesus satisfies divine justice. God's holiness demands that sin be punished, but Jesus, in His substitutionary atonement, bore the penalty in our place.

Romans 3:25 states, "God presented Christ as a sacrifice of atonement, through the shedding of His blood – to be received by faith." This means believers do not simply receive forgiveness – they receive Christ's righteousness in exchange for their sin (2 Corinthians 5:21).

Cleansing is an ongoing process. Just as the Israelites needed daily washing, believers must continually seek cleansing through repentance and the application of the blood. Jesus illustrated this concept in John 13:10 when He washed His disciples' feet and said, "The one who has bathed does not need to wash, except for his feet, but is completely clean." This indicates that while salvation is secured, believers must regularly cleanse themselves from daily impurities through confession and reliance on the blood.

Forgiveness through the blood of Jesus also restores intimacy with God. Sin creates distance, but through confession and the blood's cleansing power, believers can walk in continual fellowship with the Father. Hebrews 10:22 encourages, "Let us draw near with a sincere heart in full assurance of faith, having our hearts sprinkled clean from an evil conscience." The blood not only cleanses outward sin but also purifies the conscience, allowing believers to stand confidently before God.

3. Justification and Righteousness

The third effect of the blood of Jesus is justification. To be justified means to be declared righteous in God's sight, as if one had never sinned. Romans 5:9 states, "Since we have now been justified by his blood, how much more shall we be saved from God's wrath through him!"

Justification is a legal term that signifies acquittal. In the courtroom of heaven, Satan accuses believers day and night

(Revelation 12:10), but the blood of Jesus serves as irrefutable evidence of their innocence. The Greek word for justification, *dikaioó*, means to acquit, make right, or declare innocent. When believers stand before God, He does not see their past sins; He sees the righteousness of Christ.

Isaiah 61:10 beautifully illustrates this transformation: "I will greatly rejoice in the Lord, my soul shall be joyful in my God; for he has clothed me with the garments of salvation, he has covered me with the robe of righteousness." The blood of Jesus is the legal basis for a believer's righteousness, silencing the accusations of the enemy and giving them boldness to approach God.

Through justification, believers are given a new identity. They are no longer seen as sinners but as children of God, clothed in Christ's righteousness (2 Corinthians 5:21). This righteousness is not earned through works but is received through faith in the blood. Romans 3:23-24 affirms, "For all have sinned and fall short of the glory of God, and all are justified freely by his grace through the redemption that came by Christ Jesus."

4. Sanctification – Set Apart for God

The fourth effect of the blood of Jesus is sanctification, which means being set apart as holy. Hebrews 13:12 declares, "And so Jesus also suffered outside the city gate to make the people holy through his own blood."

Sanctification is both an instant and ongoing process. At the moment of salvation, the believer is made holy before God. However, they must also walk in sanctification daily, growing in purity and obedience. 1 Thessalonians 4:7-8 states, "For God did not call us to be impure, but to live a holy life."

In the Old Testament, priests were required to be ceremonially clean before ministering in the temple. Likewise, believers today must live set apart for God's purposes. The blood of Jesus empowers them to resist sin and walk in holiness. Romans 6:11 instructs, "Reckon yourselves to be dead indeed to sin, but alive to God in Christ Jesus our Lord." Through the blood, believers are continually transformed into the image of Christ.

Sanctification also involves separation from the world's corruption. As believers grow in their faith, they are called to reject sin and embrace God's standards of righteousness. The blood makes this transformation possible, empowering them to walk in purity and divine purpose.

5. Salvation and Eternal Life

The fifth effect of the blood of Jesus is salvation, which secures eternal life. John 3:16 famously states, "For God so loved the world that he gave his only Son, that whoever believes in him should not perish but have eternal life." Salvation is the ultimate purpose of Christ's sacrifice.

Many misunderstand salvation as merely an escape from hell, but it is much more. The Greek word *sótéria* means deliverance, healing, and preservation. Salvation through the blood of Jesus brings wholeness to every part of life – spirit, soul, and body. Romans 10:9-10 emphasizes that salvation is received through faith and confession: "If you confess with your mouth that Jesus is Lord and believe in your heart that God raised him from the dead, you will be saved."

This salvation is not just for the afterlife; it transforms the present. Jesus declared in John 10:10, "I have come that they may have life, and have it to the full." The blood of Jesus ensures victory in every area, allowing believers to walk in divine purpose and security.

6. Victory Over Satan and Spiritual Warfare

The blood of Jesus is one of the most powerful weapons in spiritual warfare, capable of breaking every stronghold of darkness. Revelation 12:11 declares, "They triumphed over him by the blood of the Lamb and by the word of their testimony." This verse reveals the key to victory: the blood of Jesus combined with spoken faith. The blood has already defeated Satan, but believers must enforce that victory by declaring it in their lives.

Satan is described as "the accuser of the brethren" (Revelation 12:10), constantly seeking to condemn and trap believers in guilt and bondage. However, the blood silences his accusations. Just as the high priest in the Old Testament sprinkled the blood of the sacrifice on the mercy seat for the forgiveness of Israel's sins, Jesus' blood now speaks on behalf of believers, ensuring that Satan's accusations are powerless. Colossians 2:15 confirms this: "Having disarmed the powers and authorities, He made a public spectacle of them, triumphing over them by the cross."

The blood of Jesus is also a shield in spiritual battles. Just as the Israelites were protected during the Passover by the lamb's blood on their doorposts (Exodus 12:13), believers today are covered and safeguarded from demonic oppression by the blood of Christ. This protection is not automatic – it must be applied by faith. Declaring, "I plead the blood of Jesus over my home, my family, and my life," reinforces divine protection, blocking spiritual attacks before they manifest.

Believers must also recognize that spiritual warfare is ongoing. While Jesus has already won the victory, the enemy continues to attack, seeking to steal, kill, and destroy (John 10:10). The enemy uses fear, temptation, and deception to weaken faith, but the blood of Jesus serves as a reminder of his ultimate defeat. The Apostle Paul urges believers to "put on the full armor of God" (Ephesians 6:11) and to "resist the devil, and he will flee" (James 4:7). A key part of this resistance is declaring the power of the blood.

Many believers have experienced deliverance from oppression, nightmares, and fear through applying the blood of Jesus in prayer. When spoken with faith, the blood disrupts the enemy's plans, dismantles spiritual attacks, and fortifies believers against demonic schemes. The blood is not just a symbol; it is an active force that drives back darkness and establishes the authority of Christ in a believer's life.

7. Healing Through the Blood

The blood of Jesus is the foundation of divine healing, bringing restoration to the body, mind, and soul. Isaiah 53:5 prophesies, "By His stripes, we are healed." This was fulfilled in the suffering of Jesus, whose body was broken so that humanity could be made whole. Healing is not just a spiritual concept – it is a covenant promise established through Christ's blood.

The connection between blood and healing is seen throughout Scripture. In Leviticus 17:11, God states, "For the life of the flesh is in the blood." Medically, blood carries oxygen, nutrients, and healing properties to every cell in the body. Spiritually, Jesus' blood carries life and restoration, reversing the effects of sin, sickness, and oppression.

Healing through the blood is not limited to physical ailments. Emotional wounds, mental health struggles, and spiritual oppression are also healed through Christ's sacrifice. Psalm 147:3 declares, "He heals the brokenhearted and binds up their wounds." Many believers have experienced freedom from depression, anxiety, and trauma by proclaiming the healing power of the blood.

Faith is a critical component of receiving healing. James 5:15 states, "The prayer of faith will save the sick, and the Lord will raise him up." Healing is not based on human effort but on the finished work of Christ. When believers declare, "By the blood of Jesus, I am healed," they activate the power of God's promises.

Countless testimonies confirm miraculous healings through the blood of Jesus. Some have been instantly healed, while others have experienced gradual restoration as they continued to proclaim the blood over their bodies. Regardless of the method, healing is available to all who believe. The blood of Jesus is still as powerful today as it was at Calvary, bringing health and wholeness to all who receive it.

8. Direct Access to God

Before the crucifixion, access to God was restricted. The high priest could only enter the Holy of Holies once a year with the blood of animal sacrifices (Hebrews 9:7). However, when Jesus died, the veil of the temple was torn from top to bottom (Matthew 27:51), signifying that the barrier between humanity and God was removed.

Hebrews 10:19-20 declares, "Therefore, brothers and sisters, since we have confidence to enter the Most Holy Place by the blood of Jesus, by a new and living way opened for us through the curtain, that is, His body." Through Christ's blood, believers now have direct access to the Father.

This means that prayer is not just a religious duty but an intimate conversation with God. Because of the blood, believers can boldly approach the throne of grace (Hebrews 4:16), knowing that they are welcomed as sons and daughters. No longer do they need an intermediary priest – Jesus is the eternal High Priest, interceding on their behalf (Romans 8:34).

Access to God through the blood of Jesus transforms worship, prayer, and daily communion with the Lord. It removes guilt and shame, allowing believers to stand before God with confidence. This direct relationship brings peace, joy, and a deeper understanding of God's love.

9. Protection from Evil

The blood of Jesus is a powerful source of divine protection against spiritual attacks, witchcraft, and demonic forces. Just as the Israelites were protected from death during the Passover (Exodus 12:13), believers today are shielded from harm when they apply the blood through faith.

Psalm 91:10 states, "No harm will overtake you, no disaster will come near your tent." The blood of Jesus acts as a spiritual barrier that the enemy cannot penetrate. Many testimonies confirm the power of the blood in protecting people from accidents, oppression, and even physical danger.

This protection is reinforced through daily proclamation. A believer who consistently declares, "I plead the blood of Jesus over my life, my family, and my home," is reinforcing a hedge of protection that the enemy cannot cross. The blood covers every area of life – health, finances, relationships, and destiny – ensuring safety from unseen forces of darkness.

10. Authority and Deliverance from Bondage

The final effect of the blood of Jesus is authority over the enemy and deliverance from bondage. Jesus' sacrifice not only forgave sins but also broke every chain of captivity. Luke 10:19 proclaims, "Behold, I give you authority to trample on serpents and scorpions, and over all the power of the enemy."

Many people struggle with generational curses, addictions, and oppressive spiritual forces. However, Jesus' blood cancels every demonic assignment. Colossians 1:13-14 declares, "For He has rescued us from the dominion of darkness and brought us into the kingdom of the Son He loves, in whom we have redemption, the forgiveness of sins."

Deliverance is accessed through faith and proclamation. Believers must declare, "By the blood of Jesus, I break every chain of bondage in my life." Demonic oppression cannot withstand the power of the blood. Every believer has been given authority to stand firm against the enemy, knowing that victory has already been won through Christ's sacrifice.

Applying the blood in spiritual warfare dismantles strongholds and frees believers from every form of bondage. Whether struggling with addiction, fear, or generational curses, the blood of Jesus provides the power to overcome. Those who understand and apply the blood experience true freedom and walk in the authority given by Christ.

**

The blood of Jesus, shed seven times on earth, works in ten transformative ways in our lives today. Under the law of Moses, no one could fully obey the ten commandments, and failure brought sin and death. The blood of Jesus, however, fulfills the law, setting us free from sin and its curse. Through grace, mercy, and love, His blood replaces the condemnation of the old covenant with the redemption of the new.

This divine mystery is rooted in the Godhead – Father, Son, and Holy Spirit as one. 1 Corinthians 15:21-28 declares, "For as in Adam all die, so in Christ all will be made alive." Death entered through Adam, but Christ's resurrection brings life. Jesus reigns until all His enemies, including death, are vanquished. When His work is complete, He will hand the kingdom to the Father, and God will be all in all.

Dr. David Jeremiah distinguishes between two races: the natural man under Adam and the spiritual man under Christ. To be in Adam is to live in the flesh; to be in Christ is to be spiritually alive (Romans 5:12-19). In the end, Christ will rule, the millennial reign will occur, and death itself will be cast into the lake of fire (Daniel 2:44, Revelation 20:14).

Prayer for the Blood of Jesus:

I cover myself, my family, my home, and my church with the blood of Jesus. Protect us from the enemy's accusations. Thank You, Lord, for Your sacrifice on the cross. Amen.

Revelation 12:11 declares, "They overcame him by the blood of the Lamb and the word of their testimony." Believers will triumph over Satan through Christ's blood and their witness, valuing eternal life above earthly gain. 1 John 2:17 reminds us, "The world is passing away... but he who does the will of God abides forever." The pleasures of this world fade, but obedience to God leads to eternal glory.

Revelation 7:16-17 promises, "Never again will they hunger or thirst... For the Lamb at the center of the throne will be their shepherd." In heaven, believers will live in everlasting joy with Christ, the Lamb who shepherds them to springs of living water (Psalm 23, Isaiah 49:10, Revelation 21:3-4).

Jesus, the second Adam, came in the flesh to restore life. Through Adam, humanity inherited sin and death; through Jesus, we inherit righteousness and eternal life. His coming is the ultimate covenant, overthrowing Satan's dominion. As believers, it is our duty to proclaim His blood, His Word, and our testimony. These three are inseparable, leading to a victorious life in Christ.

**

The blood of Jesus is the foundation of the Christian life, securing redemption, cleansing, justification, sanctification, and salvation. Yet, its effects extend beyond salvation to include victory over Satan, healing, direct access to God, protection, and deliverance.

Understanding these ten effects allows believers to walk in full confidence, knowing that every aspect of their lives is covered by the power of the blood. The enemy thrives on ignorance – many Christians fail to experience victory simply because they do not understand or apply what Christ has already provided. However, when believers apply the blood through faith and proclamation, they activate divine protection, healing, and authority.

The power of the blood is not a relic of the past; it is a present reality. It speaks on behalf of every believer, silencing the accusations of the enemy and opening the doors of heaven's blessings. The call is clear: believers must not only recognize the power of the blood but also actively apply it in every area of life.

With this understanding, the words of Revelation 12:11 take on new meaning: "They triumphed over him by the blood of the Lamb and by the word of their testimony." Victory is already won, and through the blood of Jesus, every believer can walk in complete freedom, healing, and authority.

Chapter Eleven:
Jesus: Fully Man And Fully God

"There was and is one perfect man on earth and in heaven. This man is called Jesus Christ of Nazareth. His divinity and humanity make him the unique one – God Himself incarnated in flesh."

(Monika Starova)

The mystery of Jesus' nature as both fully God and fully man is central to understanding the power of His blood and the effectiveness of His sacrifice. From the moment of His incarnation, Jesus embodied both the divine and the human, existing as the eternal Son of God while taking on flesh to walk among us. This dual nature is not merely a theological concept but a foundational truth that directly impacts every believer's faith, salvation, and relationship with God. Jesus' humanity made Him the perfect sacrifice for sin, while His divinity made that sacrifice eternal and powerful enough to redeem all of humanity. Without both aspects, His mission on earth would have been incomplete.

The love that Christ demonstrated by coming to earth in human form is beyond comprehension. John 3:16 proclaims, "For God so loved the world that he gave his one and only Son, that whoever believes in him shall not perish but have eternal life." This love surpasses human understanding because it reflects the heart of God, who was willing to send His Son into a fallen world to suffer and die for humanity's redemption. Jesus did not have to endure the cross, but in His perfect obedience to the Father, He laid down His life willingly. In doing so, He exemplified the greatest act of love the world has ever known.

Jesus' birth was unlike any other, as it was the miraculous result of divine intervention. The Gospel of Matthew declares, "The virgin will conceive and give birth to a son, and they will call him Immanuel" (Matthew 1:23). This prophecy, fulfilled in Christ, testifies to the divine nature of His incarnation. He was conceived by the Holy Spirit and born of the Virgin Mary, ensuring that He was not tainted by the sinful nature inherited from Adam. Luke 1:35 states, "The Holy Spirit will come upon you, and the power of the Most High will overshadow you. So the holy one to be born will be called the Son of God." Unlike every other human being, Jesus was without sin, making Him the only one qualified to be the spotless Lamb of God.

The necessity of Jesus' humanity is emphasized in Hebrews 2:14-17, which explains that He had to take on flesh in order to atone for humanity's sins. He experienced temptation, suffering, and the limitations of human weakness, yet remained sinless. This made Him the perfect mediator between God and man. While Adam failed and brought sin into the world, Jesus, the second Adam, succeeded where the first had fallen short. Through His obedience and sacrifice, He restored what had been lost. 2 Corinthians 5:21 affirms, "God made him who had no sin to be sin for us, so that in him we might become the righteousness of God."

The righteousness of Christ is now imparted to those who believe in Him. Because He lived a perfect life, fulfilling every requirement of the Law, His sacrifice on the cross was sufficient to redeem mankind. 1 Peter 1:19 describes Him as "a lamb without blemish or defect," underscoring the purity of His life and the completeness of His offering. His blood was not like the blood of sacrificial animals, which could only provide temporary atonement. Rather, His blood was divine, powerful, and eternal, able to cleanse sin completely and bring humanity back into right standing with God.

Jesus' life on earth was not only about His death; it was also a model of divine love, service, and obedience. Throughout His ministry, He healed the sick, cast out demons, and performed miracles, demonstrating His divine authority while also showing deep compassion for humanity. Every act of Jesus reflected the heart of the Father. John 8:29 states, "I always do what pleases Him," illustrating His perfect submission to God. This obedience was essential, for it allowed Him to become the perfect sacrifice. Had He sinned even once, His death on the cross would have been insufficient for salvation. But because He remained blameless, His sacrifice was able to secure righteousness for all who believe.

As a fully man, Jesus experienced hunger, fatigue, grief, and temptation. He wept at the death of Lazarus (John 11:35), showing His deep empathy for human suffering. He was tempted by Satan in the wilderness (Matthew 4:1-11), yet He never yielded to sin. His humanity enabled Him to relate to our struggles, making Him the perfect High Priest who understands our weaknesses. Hebrews 4:15 declares, "For we do not have a high priest who is unable to empathize with our weaknesses, but we have one who has been tempted in every way, just as we are – yet he did not sin."

Yet, despite His full humanity, Jesus never ceased to be fully God. He forgave sins (Mark 2:5-7), accepted worship (John 20:28), and declared, "Before Abraham was, I am" (John 8:58), affirming His eternal existence. His authority over nature, sickness, demons, and even death confirmed His divinity. The apostles recognized this truth, as evidenced in Thomas' exclamation, "My Lord and my God!" (John 20:28). Throughout Scripture, Jesus is revealed as both the Son of Man and the Son of God, bridging the gap between heaven and earth.

The significance of Jesus' dual nature is especially evident in His atoning work on the cross. If He had been merely human, His sacrifice would have been no different from any other person's death. But because He was also divine, His sacrifice had infinite value. His blood was not ordinary; it was pure, holy, and powerful, capable of redeeming all of humanity. Hebrews 9:12 states, "He did not enter by means of the blood of goats and calves; but he entered the Most Holy Place once for all by his own blood, thus obtaining eternal redemption."

His resurrection further validated His deity. After three days in the tomb, He rose again, proving that He had conquered sin, death, and the grave. His appearances to His disciples and followers after His resurrection demonstrated that He was both alive and victorious. He ascended to heaven, where He now sits at the right hand of the Father, interceding for believers (Romans 8:34). His divine nature ensured that His work on earth was not temporary but had eternal significance.

The dual nature of Christ is a mystery that is difficult to fully comprehend, yet it is essential to understanding the power of His blood. Without His humanity, He could not have been the perfect sacrifice. Without His divinity, His sacrifice would not have been sufficient to atone for the sins of the whole world. It is in this perfect union of God and man that salvation is made possible. His life, death, and resurrection stand as the ultimate testament to God's love, justice, and mercy.

**

Jesus' role as both fully God and fully man is not just a theological truth but a reality that shapes the entire Christian faith. His dual nature is what gives power to His sacrifice, ensuring that His blood was sufficient to redeem humanity eternally. Without His divinity, His sacrifice would have been temporary. Without His humanity, He would not have been able to take the place of mankind. His unique nature allows Him to act as both the mediator and the atonement, bringing humanity back into a right relationship with God.

Throughout His earthly ministry, Jesus demonstrated the attributes of both natures. He humbled Himself to be born into a poor family, learning obedience through the hardships of human life, yet He also displayed divine power through miracles, healings, and authority over nature. He experienced hunger and thirst, yet He multiplied loaves and fish to feed thousands. He grew weary, yet He walked on water. He wept at the sorrow of death, yet He commanded Lazarus to come out of the grave. Every moment of His life was a testimony to this mystery, where the limitations of humanity and the limitless power of divinity existed in perfect harmony.

One of the greatest evidences of His divine nature was His authority over sin. No mere human could forgive sin, yet Jesus repeatedly declared, "Your sins are forgiven" (Mark 2:5). The Pharisees were outraged by this, knowing that only God could forgive sin. But Jesus, in full knowledge of His divine identity, exercised His authority to remove the weight of guilt from sinners. The woman caught in adultery, the paralyzed man lowered through the roof, the thief on the cross – each experienced firsthand the power of Jesus' forgiveness, a power that stemmed from His divine nature. Yet, His humanity allowed Him to fully understand the struggles of those He forgave, offering them not just pardon, but compassion and restoration.

His divine authority was also evident in His dominion over demons. When confronted by unclean spirits, Jesus did not struggle or engage in elaborate rituals. He simply commanded, and they obeyed. In Mark 5, a man possessed by a legion of demons fell before Jesus, recognizing His divine authority. The demons pleaded for permission to enter a herd of pigs, knowing that they had no power against the Son of God. Unlike human prophets or priests, who had to rely on the name of the Lord for power, Jesus exercised divine authority from within Himself. His commands were final, His words carried the weight of God's own voice.

At the same time, Jesus did not separate Himself from the struggles of ordinary people. He was not a distant or untouchable deity. He walked among the outcasts, touched lepers, dined with sinners, and wept with those who mourned. He allowed Himself to feel the full weight of human sorrow, suffering betrayal, abandonment, and injustice. His humanity was not an illusion or a mere appearance – it was a lived reality. He experienced the depth of human emotion, the sting of rejection, and the weight of pain, yet He never allowed His human experience to override His divine purpose.

Nowhere was this dual nature more evident than in the Garden of Gethsemane. As He prayed before His arrest, He exhibited the tension between His human will and divine mission. "Father, if you are willing, take this cup from me; yet not my will, but yours be done"

(Luke 22:42). In this moment, His humanity felt the anguish of what lay ahead – the physical torture, the spiritual burden of bearing the world's sin, and the temporary separation from the Father. Yet, His divine submission overruled the weakness of flesh, and He willingly embraced the cross. This was not just an act of obedience; it was an act of perfect love.

His crucifixion was the ultimate expression of His dual nature. As a man, He suffered humiliation, pain, and death. He bled, He gasped for breath, He cried out in agony. But as God, His death carried infinite weight, absorbing the sins of the world and satisfying divine justice. When He declared, "It is finished" (John 19:30), it was not just a statement of relief – it was a declaration of victory. The price was paid, the curse was broken, and the work was complete. This was not the end of Jesus' life; it was the fulfillment of His mission.

Three days later, His divine power was on full display as He rose from the grave. No ordinary man could resurrect himself, but Jesus, being fully God, had authority over life and death. His resurrection confirmed that His sacrifice was accepted, that sin had been defeated, and that those who put their faith in Him would share in His victory. When He appeared to His disciples, He was not merely a spirit or a vision – He was in His resurrected, glorified body. He ate with them, spoke with them, and even invited Thomas to touch His wounds. The reality of His resurrection solidified the truth that He was both fully human and fully divine.

His ascension further affirmed this. As He was taken up into heaven, He did not shed His humanity. He remains, to this day, the God-Man, seated at the right hand of the Father. Hebrews 7:25 tells us that He "always lives to intercede" for believers. His role as High Priest is not temporary – it is eternal. He continues to act as the mediator between God and humanity, ensuring that those who trust in Him are covered by His righteousness.

Because Jesus retains His human nature, He serves as the eternal representative of redeemed humanity. He did not return to a purely spiritual form; He remains in His glorified body, a constant reminder that He is both the Lamb who was slain and the King who reigns forever. This truth has profound implications for believers. It means that the one who intercedes for them understands their struggles, their weaknesses, and their fears. He is not distant or unfamiliar with human suffering – He has lived it, and He has conquered it.

The fact that Jesus was both fully God and fully man is also crucial to understanding the power of His blood. Because He was divine, His blood carried infinite value, able to atone for all sin for all time. Because He was human, His blood was a true and fitting substitute for mankind's sin. The sacrifices of the Old Testament were repeated year after year, unable to fully cleanse sin. But Hebrews 9:12 states, "He entered the Most Holy Place once for all by His own blood, thus obtaining eternal redemption." His sacrifice does not need to be repeated. It was final, complete, and forever effective.

In more recent times, some have even claimed physical evidence of this mystery. The archaeologist Ron Wyatt reported in the 1980s that while working near Golgotha, he discovered traces of what he believed to be the blood of Christ. According to his account, laboratory testing revealed something extraordinary: the blood was still living, not dead, and it carried only twenty-four chromosomes. Unlike ordinary human blood, which has forty-six chromosomes—twenty-three from each parent—this sample was said to have twenty-three human chromosomes and one that was not human. For Wyatt, this served as a striking confirmation of the faith's central claim: that Jesus was fully human, receiving His humanity from His mother, and yet also fully divine, bearing the mark of God Himself. Though controversial, the story has often been used to illustrate the unique and supernatural nature of Christ's blood, which purifies, forgives, and redeems.

The implications of this truth are staggering. It means that every person who places their faith in Jesus is covered by His sacrifice, no matter their past, no matter their failures. It means that believers are not merely forgiven – they are justified, made righteous before God. It means that the separation between humanity and God has been bridged forever. And it means that one day, those who belong to Christ will share in His resurrection, receiving glorified bodies just as He did.

Understanding the dual nature of Jesus deepens the believer's faith, strengthening their confidence in His ability to save, heal, and restore. He is not just a historical figure or a wise teacher – He is the eternal Son of God, who took on flesh to redeem mankind. He is the Lion and the Lamb, the Judge and the Savior, the Creator and the Redeemer. His identity is the foundation of the Christian faith, the reason for hope, and the guarantee of eternal life.

Chapter Twelve: The Blood And The Church Today

"The church of today should accept everyone-every soul, every human being, whatever denomination or religious background–willing to partake in the Holy Communion, the Eucharist."

(Monika Starova)

The church today continues to operate under the power of the blood of Jesus, which remains as relevant now as it was in the early days of Christianity. The blood is central to every aspect of faith, from worship and prayer to deliverance and healing. It is through the blood that believers find unity, redemption, and protection.

Leviticus 8:22-26 shows us a powerful moment in the Old Testament where blood was applied as part of consecrating Aaron and his sons into priestly service. The ritual included placing blood on the right ear, thumb, and big toe of each man, symbolizing total consecration – what they heard, what they did, and where they walked.

This symbolic act was foundational to the priesthood's sanctification and service in God's presence.

Today, the church is called a royal priesthood (1 Peter 2:9), and while we no longer perform animal sacrifices, the principle of being marked and set apart by blood still stands. The blood of Jesus spiritually consecrates modern believers in the same comprehensive way: cleansing our hearing (spiritual discernment), our hands (our work and actions), and our feet (our walk and conduct). It is a reminder that our entire lives are to be marked and led by the redeeming blood of Christ. Churches that understand and actively apply the power of the blood experience revival, strength, and victory over darkness. The shedding of Jesus' blood was not just an event in history; it is a continual source of life, renewal, and transformation for the body of Christ.

One of the most significant ways the church acknowledges the blood of Jesus today is through the practice of communion. During the Last Supper, Jesus established the ordinance of the Eucharist, instructing His disciples to drink the cup in remembrance of Him. This act symbolizes participation in the new covenant, sealed by His blood. When churches, including pastors and priests, partake in communion, they are reaffirming their dependence on the blood of Christ for salvation, unity, and spiritual nourishment. 1 Corinthians 10:16 states, "The cup of blessing that we bless, is it not a participation in the blood of Christ?" This means that every time believers drink from the cup, they are spiritually engaging with the life-giving power of His sacrifice. Communion is not merely a ritual; it is a declaration of faith, a proclamation of victory, and an affirmation of the believer's connection to Christ.

Beyond communion, churches today apply the blood of Jesus in their prayers, recognizing it as a powerful force in spiritual warfare. Many believers incorporate the blood into their daily prayers, pleading it over their families, homes, and workplaces for divine protection. The early church understood the importance of prayer and covering themselves with the blood, and this practice continues in the modern church. Pastors, priests, and intercessors often lead congregations in proclaiming the blood over their lives, following the biblical principle that "they overcame him by the blood of the Lamb and by the word of their testimony" (Revelation 12:11). When believers invoke the blood of Jesus, they are reminding the enemy of his defeat and standing in the authority given to them through Christ.

Spiritual warfare remains a crucial aspect of church ministry, and the blood of Jesus is a weapon that no force of darkness can withstand. Demonic forces tremble at the mention of the blood because it represents the ultimate victory of Christ over sin and death. Deliverance ministries, which focus on freeing individuals from demonic oppression, often rely on the power of the blood to break curses, cancel demonic assignments, and liberate captives. When pastors and prayer warriors command demons to flee in the name of Jesus and through His blood, they are enforcing the spiritual authority that was won at the cross. This is why testimonies of deliverance are common in churches that actively apply the blood in their ministry. People who have suffered from generational curses, witchcraft, or demonic attacks often experience complete freedom when they submit to Christ and claim the power of His blood over their lives.

The blood of Jesus also plays a significant role in healing ministries. Just as His blood provides redemption from sin, it also brings healing to the body, soul, and spirit. Isaiah 53:5 declares, "By His stripes, we are healed." Churches that emphasize healing often encourage believers to declare the blood of Jesus over their illnesses, trusting that the same power that forgives sin also restores health. Many testimonies exist of people who were miraculously healed after pleading the blood over their condition and standing in faith. Whether in physical sickness, emotional wounds, or spiritual oppression, the blood remains the ultimate remedy, bringing restoration to every part of a person's life.

One of the most crucial aspects of the blood in the church today is its role in unifying the body of Christ. The church is made up of people from different backgrounds, cultures, and denominations, yet the blood of Jesus unites them as one family. Ephesians 2:13 states, "But now in Christ Jesus you who once were far away have been brought near by the blood of Christ." This means that all who believe, regardless of their past, are brought into the same covenant and inheritance through the blood. Division within the church often arises when believers lose sight of this unifying power. When the blood of Jesus is central, there is no room for discrimination, superiority, or division. The blood calls every believer to humility, love, and oneness in Christ.

Unfortunately, some churches today have distanced themselves from the teachings on the blood, treating it as a mere theological concept rather than a present reality. This has led to a decline in spiritual power and authority in many congregations. A church that neglects the blood loses its strength because it disconnects from the source of its victory. Revival movements throughout history have often been marked by a return to the preaching and application of the blood. When believers fully grasp the power of the blood and apply it with faith, they experience supernatural breakthroughs, renewed passion for Christ, and a deeper intimacy with God. The church must return to emphasizing the blood in its teachings, worship, and daily practice, for it is the foundation of everything that defines the Christian faith.

In worship, the power of the blood should be acknowledged through songs, declarations, and thanksgiving. Hymns and contemporary worship songs that focus on the blood remind believers of its significance and keep their faith strong. The early church continually praised God for the blood, understanding that it was their source of salvation and protection. When churches today center their worship around the blood, they invite the presence of God into their midst. The blood is a doorway to divine encounters, and when believers worship with this understanding, they experience deep spiritual renewal.

The blood of Jesus is also essential in restoring churches that have fallen into spiritual complacency or corruption. Many churches today struggle with lukewarm faith, worldliness, and moral compromise. The remedy for this is a renewed focus on the blood, which cleanses, purifies, and revives. Just as the Israelites had to apply the blood of the lamb to their doorposts to be spared from judgment, churches must apply the blood of Jesus through repentance and faith to be delivered from spiritual stagnation. A church that constantly applies the blood in its teachings and practices will remain vibrant, full of the Holy Spirit, and effective in its mission.

Churches must also recognize that the blood is not just for individual believers but for entire communities. The early church was known for its radical love, generosity, and commitment to one another, all of which were rooted in the understanding that they were bound together by the blood of Christ. There should be no division in partaking of the Eucharist; all people should be welcome in churches to receive communion. Today's church must return to this mindset, seeing each other as family rather than just members of the same congregation. The blood of Jesus calls believers to care for one another, support the weak, and build each other up in faith. When the church functions as a unified body under the blood, it becomes an unstoppable force for God's kingdom.

The power of the blood should also be proclaimed boldly in evangelism. Many people are lost and in bondage, not realizing that the price for their freedom has already been paid. The church has a responsibility to share this message, bringing hope to the broken and salvation to the lost. The gospel is centered on the blood, and when churches emphasize this in their outreach, they see lives transformed. People need to hear that the blood of Jesus redeems them, forgives them, and gives them a new identity. The blood is the message of hope that the world desperately needs.

The church cannot afford to remain silent about the power of the blood of Jesus. Every sermon, every prayer meeting, every worship service should, in some way, reflect the reality that the blood is at the very core of the Christian faith. Without the blood, there is no remission of sins, no reconciliation with God, no deliverance from darkness. It is the blood that makes the gospel truly good news. Churches that preach the blood without hesitation witness greater spiritual breakthroughs, healings, and deliverances. When people understand what the blood of Jesus has done for them, they are set free from guilt, condemnation, and fear. They no longer struggle under the weight of past sins but walk in the confidence of their redemption.

**

The blood is not just a theological concept; it is a living, active force in the spiritual realm. It speaks, intercedes, and covers those who apply it by faith. When believers declare the blood over their lives, they are not engaging in empty tradition but are aligning themselves with a divine reality that has the power to transform circumstances. This is why spiritual leaders must train their congregations to actively apply the blood in their daily lives. The church should not be a place of passive spectatorship but of active engagement in the spiritual war that rages around us. Through the blood, believers are equipped with the most powerful weapon against the forces of darkness. They do not fight for victory; they fight from a place of victory, knowing that the battle has already been won through the sacrifice of Christ.

The presence of the blood is what makes the church different from any other gathering of people. It is not just a social organization or a place for moral instruction. The church is a spiritual body, infused with the life and power of Christ Himself. And that life comes through the blood. The reason the early church walked in such great authority and saw such miraculous signs and wonders was that they understood the significance of the blood. They did not rely on human wisdom or religious rituals but on the supernatural power of the blood. The same is possible today if the church returns to this foundation and refuses to dilute the message of the cross. The blood must be at the center of every teaching, every act of ministry, every step of faith.

The blood of Jesus is also the answer to the growing complacency and spiritual weakness that many churches face today. Too often, churches become comfortable with religious traditions while losing their spiritual fervor. They may have polished programs, impressive worship teams, and well-structured ministries, but without the presence of the blood, there is no real power. Many churches have abandoned deep prayer, fasting, and intercession, instead replacing them with surface-level teachings that do not challenge or equip believers for battle. This has allowed the enemy to infiltrate, bringing division, confusion, and lukewarm faith. The remedy is a return to the blood. When the church begins to proclaim the blood again, the fire of revival is rekindled. The atmosphere changes, and spiritual hunger is stirred once more. The blood is what awakens sleeping believers and calls them back into passionate pursuit of God.

Throughout history, every major revival has been marked by a renewed understanding of the blood of Jesus. When people grasp the reality of what the blood has done for them, they cannot remain passive. They fall on their knees in repentance, surrendering every part of their lives to Christ. They pray with boldness, knowing they have been given direct access to the throne of grace. They worship with deep gratitude, aware that they have been bought at a price. This is what the church today must return to. The modern church needs revival, and true revival is always birthed in the power of the blood. It is only when believers fully embrace the blood that they begin to experience the supernatural move of God in their midst.

The blood also unifies the church in a way that nothing else can. In a time when divisions and conflicts are common, the church must remember that all believers stand equal before God because of the blood. There is no higher or lower status in the kingdom of God. The blood has made all who believe into one body, regardless of nationality, background, or denomination. The enemy thrives on division because a divided church is a weakened church. But when believers understand that they are bound together by the blood, they refuse to let petty differences separate them. They stand together as one army, covered by the same blood, fighting the same battles, and proclaiming the same victory. This is why churches must continually emphasize unity through the blood. When division arises, leaders must remind their congregations that they have been reconciled not only to God but also to one another through the blood of Christ.

The church must also ensure that future generations understand the significance of the blood. There is a great responsibility to pass down this truth so that it is never lost. Parents must teach their children to apply the blood in prayer, to understand its power in their daily lives, and to live in the confidence that comes from knowing they are redeemed. Sunday schools and youth ministries must not shy away from teaching the full gospel, including the power of the blood. If the message of the blood is not firmly rooted in the hearts of young believers, they will grow up with a faith that lacks true power. They will be vulnerable to deception and spiritual attack because they do not know the authority they have in Christ. The next generation must rise up as warriors, fully aware of the power they carry because of the blood of Jesus.

The blood of Jesus is also deeply tied to the church's mission of healing and restoration. In a world filled with brokenness, pain, and despair, the church must be a place where people can come and find hope through the blood. There are many who feel too ashamed of their past to come to God, believing they are beyond redemption. But the blood declares otherwise. The church must be the voice that tells them there is no sin too great, no past too dark, that cannot be cleansed by the blood of Christ. Healing services, altar calls, and counseling sessions should all emphasize the power of the blood to restore what has been broken. The blood does not just forgive sin; it heals emotional wounds, mends relationships, and gives people a new beginning. The church is called to be a beacon of hope, pointing the lost and hurting to the cleansing power of the blood.

Ultimately, the church must never grow tired of proclaiming the blood of Jesus. It is not an outdated doctrine or a secondary issue. It is the very foundation of the Christian faith. Without the blood, there is no salvation, no victory, and no hope. Every sermon, every prayer meeting, every outreach effort should be infused with the truth of the blood. When the blood is preached, chains are broken. When the blood is declared, the enemy flees. When the blood is applied, healing flows. When the blood is at the center, the church thrives. It is time for the church to rise up in the power of the blood, to reclaim its authority, and to walk in the fullness of everything Christ has made available through His sacrifice. The blood is still speaking, still working, still redeeming. The church must continue to declare it boldly, without compromise, knowing that in the blood of Jesus, there is ultimate and eternal victory.

Chapter Thirteen:
The Legacy Of The Blood: Eternal Life & Beyond

"The legacy of the blood of Jesus is the heart of the Bible from the Old Testament to the New Testament, which will never die. It has unlimited power."

(Monika Starova)

The legacy of the blood of Jesus is one that transcends time and space, offering not only redemption and healing in our present lives but also a promise of eternal life and an inheritance that extends far beyond our earthly existence. As I reflect on the journey of faith described throughout this book, I see that the blood of Christ is the central thread that weaves together every promise, every miracle, and every testimony of salvation. It is the divine currency that paid the ultimate price for our sins and continues to secure our future with the Father. The sacrifice of Jesus on the cross was the moment when the eternal plan of God was set in motion – a plan that guarantees that those who believe in Him will receive life that never ends.

This promise of eternal life is not simply a future hope but a present reality that transforms our everyday existence. When we declare that we are redeemed by His blood, we are declaring that we are no longer bound by the limitations of this world. The blood of Jesus secures for us an eternal inheritance, a spiritual wealth that cannot be measured by earthly standards. In Romans 6:23, it is written, "For the wages of sin is death, but the gift of God is eternal life in Christ Jesus our Lord." This gift, freely given by God, assures us that our relationship with Him is not temporary; it is eternal. We have been purchased with a price that far exceeds anything we could ever imagine, and that price was the precious, unblemished blood of our Savior.

Every aspect of our lives is touched by this legacy. It is not just a historical event, nor is it confined to the pages of Scripture – it is alive and active in our hearts today. The blood of Jesus has the power to change destinies, mend broken relationships, and restore hope where despair once reigned. I have witnessed its transformative power in my own life and in the lives of countless others. For many, the application of the blood has brought healing from physical, emotional, and spiritual afflictions, providing a profound sense of peace and assurance. It has broken chains of addiction, released families from generational curses, and provided a firm foundation upon which to build a life of victory.

There is a unique intimacy that comes from embracing the truth of the blood. When we come before God in prayer and confession, we are reminded that we are not defined by our past sins, our failures, or even by the relentless accusations of the enemy. The blood speaks for us; it testifies to our freedom and victory. It is as if every drop of

Christ's blood, shed on the cross, whispers in our hearts that we are loved, redeemed, and forever secure in His grace. This is the power that fuels our hope and our determination to live a life that reflects His love and mercy. The legacy of the blood is evident in the way our lives change, how we overcome obstacles, and how we witness to others. When we boldly proclaim, "I am covered by the blood of Jesus," we are not merely reciting words – we are activating a divine reality that transforms our very being.

It is essential for us, as believers, to recognize that our eternal legacy is also a call to leave behind a heritage of faith for future generations. The power of the blood is not meant to be hoarded for our own benefit; it is a treasure that must be passed on to our children, our communities, and even to those who have yet to hear the gospel. As we live each day in the light of this truth, we become living testimonies of God's redemptive work. Our lives are to be a beacon of hope and a reminder of the unfathomable love that our Savior has for us. We are called to model a life of obedience, to walk in humility and boldness, and to use our words and actions to proclaim the truth that the blood of Jesus secures our future.

In the legacy of the blood, we find the assurance that nothing can separate us from the love of God. The promise of eternal life, secured by His sacrifice, is a legacy that overcomes sin, death, and every form of darkness. It is the ultimate victory that assures us that even when our earthly journey comes to an end, our souls will dwell forever in the presence of our Heavenly Father. The blood of Jesus, shed on the cross, is the seal of our redemption and the mark of our eternal inheritance. This is not a promise that fades with time; it is an everlasting covenant that has been established by the very power of God.

For those who may still struggle to understand the magnitude of this legacy, I offer my personal testimony. In my own life, I have seen the blood of Jesus work miracles. There were moments when I felt overwhelmed by the weight of my past, by the guilt of my sins, and by the constant attacks of the enemy. Yet, every time I cried out to God, declaring the power of His blood, I experienced breakthroughs. The chains that once held me back were shattered, and I found new strength and purpose. This was not just a matter of emotional relief, but a radical transformation that redefined my entire existence. The blood of Jesus brought healing to my wounds, both seen and unseen, and it continues to inspire me to live a life of worship and gratitude. I stand as living proof that the legacy of the blood is not merely an abstract concept – it is a vibrant, active force that reclaims and renews every part of our lives.

The church, as the body of Christ, bears this legacy as well. When we gather together in worship, when we partake in communion, when we lift our voices in prayer, we are participating in a sacred tradition that stretches back through the ages. The blood of Jesus unites us, making us one in spirit and purpose. It breaks down the walls of division, uniting believers from every nation, tribe, and tongue. In a world that is often fractured by conflict and strife, the blood offers a powerful counterpoint – a unifying force that brings harmony, healing, and hope. As we stand together, clothed in the righteousness of Christ, we are empowered to face any challenge that comes our way.

Moreover, the legacy of the blood carries with it the promise of restoration. No matter how far we may have strayed or how deep our wounds may be, the blood of Jesus calls us back to God. It redeems our past, heals our present, and secures our future. There is no sin too great, no failure too catastrophic, that cannot be overcome by the blood of Christ. This assurance is the cornerstone of our faith and the driving force behind our hope. We live with the confidence that our salvation is secure, that our future is bright, and that we are destined to inherit a glory that far exceeds our present circumstances.

The eternal significance of the blood of Jesus is a legacy that continues to impact lives in profound ways. As we consider the full scope of what His blood has accomplished – from the redemption of our souls to the transformation of our daily lives – we are called to embrace this truth wholeheartedly. The legacy of the blood is a legacy of victory over sin and death, a legacy of unconditional love and grace, and a legacy of eternal life. It is a legacy that we, as believers, are entrusted with and that we must pass on to the next generation.

**

In this final reflection on the blood of Jesus, we see that its power is not confined to the pages of Scripture or the annals of church history; it is a living force that continues to work in and through us. Every time we declare, "I am redeemed by the blood of Jesus," every time we partake in communion, every time we pray and proclaim His blood over our lives, we are not only affirming our faith but also activating a divine promise that will endure for eternity. The blood of Jesus is the cornerstone of our faith – it is the gift that grants us eternal life, the power that breaks every chain, and the love that sustains us through every trial.

As we move forward, let us leave behind a legacy of faith that is defined by our understanding and application of the blood. May we be remembered not for our achievements or our accolades, but for the way we lived in the power of the blood – united in love, transformed by grace, and victorious over every force of darkness. In this legacy, we find the true meaning of eternal life – a life that begins in the here and now and continues into the eternal presence of our Lord.

Chapter Fourteen: Prayers Of Proclamation

"The word of God and the blood of Jesus are spiritual twins; inseparable and interdependent. The blood has power, but it must be proclaimed to be activated."

(Monika Starova)

The ark of the covenant was made according to God's instructions and was placed inside the tabernacle. The lid of the ark is called the mercy seat. The Greek word is *hilasterion*, which means "the place where sin is covered." Every year, the high priest would go into the Most Holy Place and pour the blood of an animal on the golden lid of the ark. This was the mercy of God covering the sins of the people.

The solid gold lid of the ark represents the cross where the blood of Jesus Christ was poured out. The blood of Jesus, by His perfect sacrifice, brings us grace and mercy. The mercy seat was the only seat in the entire tabernacle, and God sat on it in mercy, not in judgment.

God still speaks to us from a place of mercy. The work of Christ on the cross means there is blood for us and mercy for us. I always envision Christ in heaven, in the temple, where He drops His blood on the mercy seat for us and intercedes on our behalf. Every time we pray, I imagine Jesus holding a bowl of incense—which represents our prayers—in one hand, and in the other, a bowl from which He sprinkles His precious blood on the mercy seat for us. This is what happens each time we pray: the blood of Jesus speaks for us and intercedes with the Father, so that our prayers may be answered. Today, God still provides a way to meet with us, just as He did in the Old Testament when He told the Israelites that He would meet with His people between the cherubim, on the seat of mercy.

When Jesus rose from the dead, He told Mary Magdalene, "Do not cling to Me, for I have not yet ascended to My Father" (John 20:17). These words reveal that His redemptive work was not yet complete until He carried His own blood into the heavenly sanctuary. As the true High Priest, Christ entered the heavenly tabernacle and sprinkled His blood on the mercy seat in heaven, once for all, securing eternal redemption for us. Just as the high priest sprinkled the blood of animals on the ark in the earthly temple, Jesus presented His own spotless blood in the true temple of heaven. This is why His blood continues to speak—not only on earth through our prayers, but also in heaven itself, where it testifies on our behalf before the Father.

The tabernacle is a Messianic symbol of the new covenant of Jesus, the Passover Lamb. He offered Himself as a sacrifice, replacing the need for animal sacrifices once and for all. The ancient tabernacle was a foreshadowing of Jesus Christ. I believe Christ's life, death, and resurrection show the path that leads us to the Father in heaven.

This understanding leads us into a deeper kind of prayer—one grounded in faith and spiritual authority. This is an example of a prayer you might pray at home with faith to resolve any kind of issue or problem caused by the devil or by our rebellion against God. The good news is that God is always there to forgive us and grant us mercy to help us in our time of need. As the Bible says, we must hold on to our confession in order to obtain grace and mercy.

However, we must fulfill certain conditions. First, we must be humble and respectful toward God. We must ask for forgiveness and plead the blood of Jesus over our body, soul, mind, will, and spirit. Once we have done this, we can boldly go to the courts of heaven and present our concerns to the Most High God and to our mediator, Jesus Christ. We must remember that the court of heaven is real. It is more powerful than earthly courts and is highly organized. The Judge is not a human being, but the Creator of the universe—the Almighty God. My advice is that before praying in the courts of heaven, you should be prepared and organize your petitions on paper to avoid mistakes. Satan has no legal right to attack or accuse us. Yet we must be aware that one of Satan's titles is "the accuser." Revelation 12 tells us that he accuses God's people day and night in the courts of heaven (Job 2:16; Revelation 12:10).

Here is an example of a prayer of proclamation:

Thank you, Jesus, that Your blood is pleading for us in Heaven continually. Father, in the name of Jesus Christ, Your Son, I humbly come into Your presence. In the name of Jesus, I ask that You allow me to come before Your throne as Judge of the universe. I ask that You grant me a court hearing. I am asking You to judge between my case and Satan. Therefore, I petition that You summon Satan to be present for this hearing.

Father, I dare to come before You only by the covering of the precious blood of Jesus. I have no righteousness of my own; I only have the righteousness of Your Son. Dear Father, I ask You to accept me in the courts of heaven because of the blood of Jesus. I am made righteous and justified (Romans 3:21-31).

According to Ephesians 2:18, I have access to the Father by the mediator Jesus Christ, the cornerstone. I approach the throne of God with boldness because of His grace and mercy in my time of need (Hebrews 4:16). Dear Lord, as I am accepted in the court of heaven, according to Daniel 7:10, I ask You to call all the 24 elders so they may sit as jurors for my case, and that my book be opened. I thank You, Lord Jesus, that as my advocate, You are arguing my case in the presence of Satan, God, and all 24 elders seated in the court.

Father, I have several petitions that I want to present to You in the name of Jesus.

First, I ask that You judge once and for all. I know from Your Word that You allow Satan to sift us, but I also know that the sifting comes to an end. Jesus told Peter that He had prayed for him—that after Peter was sifted, he would be strengthened and would bring comfort to others (Luke 22:31-32). Father, I humbly ask You to bring to a complete end the sifting process in our lives. I ask that You bring it to a full stop. Lord, if You have judged that You have called us into ministry and our hearts have been unwilling to obey You, then I ask that You stop Satan from testing and sifting us so we can move forward in the work You have called us to do. We are unable to fully perform what You have called us to do while we are being sifted.

Secondly, Father, I ask that You review our finances, our marriage, and our health. I ask You to judge whether we have been righteous in these areas. If Your judgment is that we have, then please hear my petition with favor, mercy, and grace through the blood of Jesus. I also ask that You make Satan remove his hands from our finances, our marriage, and our health. Lord, it is our desire to move forward in the work we believe You have called us to. Therefore, I ask that You bind Satan and his servants away from our finances, our marriage situation, and our health situation, and that You bless us in these areas.

Thank You, Lord, for giving me the opportunity to present my case and to hear Jesus, my mediator. Thank You for setting me free from the bondages and troubles I have experienced in my finances, marriage, and health. You have made a way of victory in my life because of the blood of Jesus, which speaks of mercy and grace. In the name of Jesus, I thank You, Lord, for hearing and favoring my case. Amen.

As we continue in prayer and faith, we recognize the power of proclaiming the blood of Jesus over our lives. Lord Jesus, I do believe that You died on Calvary for my sins. I have sinned against You. I am sorry, and I ask You to forgive me. I ask You to be my Savior. I do not fully understand everything, but I believe it is not by my good works, but by Your great work at Calvary that I am saved.

When we accept Jesus and His sacrificial blood, our names are written in the Book of Life. We become children of God, and we have a great High Priest forever. The act of proclamation becomes very powerful in our lives when we do it in faith. As the teacher and pastor Derek Prince once said, "Confessing strengthens believing; believing strengthens confessing." The more we confess, the more we believe—and the more we believe, the more we confess.

As the apostle Paul wrote in Hebrews 10:20-24, it is important to confess the Word of God in our lives because we have Jesus as our High Priest. We must hold fast to our confession, meaning we continue to speak it without wavering, even when the forces of darkness try to hinder us. As believers in Christ, we are in spiritual warfare against the enemy—the devil, his demons, and the evil spirits of darkness. Paul writes, "By a new and living way which He consecrated for us, through the veil, that is, His flesh, and having a High Priest over the house of God, let us draw near with a true heart in full assurance of faith, having our hearts sprinkled from an evil conscience and our bodies washed with pure water. Let us hold fast the confession of our hope without wavering, for He who promised is faithful" (Hebrews 10:20-24).

When we hold fast our confession in faith, we are grounded in the hope of Christ. Faith and confession are inseparable. As James 2:17 reminds us, "Thus also faith by itself, if it does not have works, is dead." This means that while we proclaim our faith with our words, we must also act according to the Word of God. Our actions must align with our confession. This includes maintaining a positive attitude, encouraging one another, and rejecting negativity and despair. The Holy Spirit guides us to the right actions and empowers us to act in faith.

Being grateful and thankful to God is one of the most powerful ways to act out our proclamation. In 1 Thessalonians 5:18 (NKJV), it says, "In everything give thanks; for this is the will of God in Christ Jesus for you." I have realized in my own life that when I am grateful to God in everything—thanking Him daily and not complaining—breakthroughs happen in even the most difficult situations. I have witnessed many miracles: the protection of my family during the civil war in Albania, healing for my sick mother, and my own journey to Canada. All of this came through giving thanks and being grateful, even when it was hard.

Even Jesus, who was God Himself, gave thanks before performing miracles. When feeding the 5,000 with just two fish and five loaves of bread, He didn't pray—He simply gave thanks. As we read in John 6:11, "And Jesus took the loaves, and when He had given thanks, He distributed them to the disciples, and the disciples to those sitting down; and likewise of the fish, as much as they wanted."

We see that the miracle of Jesus feeding the multitude took place after He gave thanks to the Father for the five loaves and two fish. This act of gratitude unlocked the supernatural. In Hebrews 3:1 (NIV), it says, "Therefore, holy brothers and sisters, who share in the heavenly calling, fix your thoughts on Jesus, whom we acknowledge as our apostle and high priest." Jesus is the High Priest of our confession. This verse shows that right confession is vital for believers. When we speak in alignment with God's Word, we invite Jesus to be our High Priest, our mediator, and our advocate in the courts of Heaven.

The words of our confession shape our lives and destinies. When we speak in faith and truth, Jesus stands with us and intercedes on our behalf. But when we speak negatively or contrary to God's Word, we give the enemy room to influence and even destroy areas of our lives. The mouth is powerful. As Proverbs 18:21 says, "Death and life are in the power of the tongue." Our words can either bring life or bring destruction.

Words rooted in Scripture build up, bless, and bring healing, not only to others but also to ourselves. But when our speech contradicts the truth of the Bible, it can lead to calamity, damage, and even spiritual death. Matthew 12:37 (NKJV) powerfully reminds us, "For by your words you will be justified, and by your words you will be condemned." This verse speaks deeply to me. Even after becoming a Christian, there were times when I spoke negatively, out of anger, frustration, or disappointment. I saw firsthand how those words had consequences in my life and my family. Whenever I spoke against others or spoke defeat over myself, those words, empowered by unseen spiritual forces, created real damage.

The power of the tongue is also described by James in Scripture. He uses a strong metaphor to compare the tongue to a fire. In James 3:5-6 (NKJV), he writes, "See how great a forest a little fire kindles! And the tongue is a fire, a world of iniquity." When we speak words that are not in line with God's truth, they can cause great harm, both to others and to ourselves. Once released, those words are difficult to take back.

To combat this, we proclaim the truth of the blood of Jesus over our lives. You might begin with a declaration like this: *I, Monika Starova, am free from the curse of sin by the blood of Jesus Christ. I am untouchable by the blood of Jesus—on earth and on the way to the Father's throne.*

**

Redemption
Ephesians 1:7 – "In Him we have redemption through His blood, the forgiveness of sins, according to the riches of His grace." Prayer: Thank You, God, because through Your blood I have redemption, the forgiveness of my sins, according to the riches of Your grace.

Forgiveness
Through the blood of Jesus Christ, my sin is forgiven. I have been redeemed from the hand of the Devil.

1 John 1:9 (NKJV) – "If we confess our sins, He is faithful and just to forgive us our sins and to cleanse us from all unrighteousness."

Psalm 107:2 – "Let the redeemed of the Lord say so."

Cleansing

1 John 1:7 – "But if we walk in the light, as He is in the light, we have fellowship with one another, and the blood of Jesus, His Son, cleanses us from all sin."

As I walk in the light, the blood of Jesus is cleansing me now and continually from all sin. Thank You, Lord, because as I walk in the light, as You are in the light, and as I fellowship with my brothers and sisters in the church, Your blood cleanses me from all sin. Amen.

Sanctification

Hebrews 10:10 (NKJV) – "By that will we have been sanctified through the offering of the body of Jesus Christ once for all." Thank You, Jesus, because I am sanctified and made holy by the offering of the blood of Jesus Christ. Through the blood of Jesus, I'm sanctified, set apart to God, and made holy as Jesus is holy. Through the blood of Jesus, I'm sanctified, made holy, and set apart to God. The devil has no place in me, no power over me, and no unsettled plans toward me, as everything has been settled by the blood of Jesus.

Justification

Romans 5:8-9 – "But God demonstrates His own love toward us, in that while we were still sinners, Christ died for us. Much more than having now been justified by His blood, we shall be saved from wrath through Him."

Through the blood of Jesus, I am justified just as if I had never sinned. Thank You, Lord, because of Your love, You shed Your blood for me, and I am justified, made righteous as though I have never sinned, by Your blood.

Healing

Isaiah 53:5 – "But He was pierced for our transgressions, He was crushed for our iniquities; the punishment that brought us peace was upon Him, and by His wounds we are healed."

Thank You, Lord, because You were crushed for my iniquities, You were bruised for my transgressions, and by Your wounds, I am healed.
1 Peter 2:24 (NKJV) – "Who Himself bore our sins in His own body on the tree, that we, having died to sins, might live for righteousness—by whose stripes you were healed."

Thank You, Lord Jesus, because on the Cross, You bore my sins. I died to my sins, and I live for righteousness, and by Your stripes, I was healed.

Access into Heaven

Hebrews 10:19 (NIV) – "Therefore, brethren, having boldness to enter the Holiest by the blood of Jesus." Thank You, God, that through the sprinkled blood of Jesus, I have access into Your presence, the presence of the Mighty God, into the holy place in all the universes.

Thank You, Lord, that even when I cannot pray, the blood of Jesus is pleading for me in Heaven.

Victory and Protection

Revelation 12:11 (NKJV) – "And they overcame him by the blood of the Lamb and by the word of their testimony, and they did not love their lives to the death."

Thank You, Lord, that through the blood of Jesus and our words of testimony, our proclamation, we overcome Satan and his angels once and for all. We have victory in Christ. Amen.
1 John 2:1-2 (NKJV) – "My little children, these things I write to you, so that you may not sin. And if anyone sins, we have an Advocate with the Father, Jesus Christ the righteous. And He Himself is the

propitiation for our sins, and not for ours only, but also for the whole world."

Thank You, Lord, because when I sin and I come in repentance toward You, covering myself with Your blood, Jesus is my Advocate before the throne of God, and I am made holy and righteous because Jesus is righteous.

Deliverance from Bondage

Hebrews 2:14 – "That through death He might destroy him who had the power of death, that is, the devil, and release those who through fear of death were all their lifetime subject to bondage." Thank You, Lord, that the blood of Jesus has destroyed the devil and the power of death, and I am no longer subject to bondage. The blood of Jesus has broken the chains of bondage over me and my family, setting us free. I am delivered from the bondage of sin and generational curses in Jesus' name, by the blood of Jesus. Romans 7:6 – "Now we have been delivered from the law." Thank You, Jesus, that I am delivered from the law. Romans 6:6 (NKJV) – "Knowing this, that our old man was crucified with Him, that the body of sin might be done away with, that we should no longer be slaves of sin." Thank You, Lord, for delivering me from my fleshly nature because of what Jesus has done on the Cross for me. Amen!

Life / Eternal Life

Romans 6:23 – "For the wages of sin is death, but the gift of God is eternal life in Christ Jesus our Lord." Thank You, Lord, because of Your bloodshed on Calvary, You have given me eternal life. There is salvation for our souls after our bodily death through the blood of Christ. Amen. Thank You, Lord, because of the blood of Jesus, I have obtained eternal life for my soul—the life of Christ, everlasting and glorious. Amen.

**

In this truth, we stand firm and bold against every chain the prince of darkness has tried to place over our lives, our families, and our marriages. We now step into a dimension where God Himself becomes our liberator.

Conclusion

The reason I wrote this book is deeply personal. On the morning of January 1, 2009, the Lord Jesus Christ appeared to me in a dream. In this dream, I found myself present during the crucifixion of our Lord, witnessing the process as Roman soldiers and Jewish people carried out the horrific act. I could feel and see the immense suffering Jesus endured, His blood being poured out for the redemption of humanity. As I watched, every drop of His precious blood was sacrificed for our sins.

When the soldier pierced His side, the last of His blood and water poured out. The suffering of the Lord Jesus Christ – how He was beaten, tortured, rejected, and humiliated – was shown to me in the dream as a powerful expression of God's amazing, inexplicable, and mysterious love for all of humanity. Jesus was as much God as He was man, and He humbled Himself, surrendering His will. He did not resist the torture and punishment on the cross, knowing that it was essential for the will of the Father to be fulfilled.

Jesus shed His blood seven times during His crucifixion. Each drop of His blood holds immense power in our daily lives: it brings redemption, eternal life, sanctification, righteousness, justification, salvation, the Holy Spirit, and the power to break free from bondage.

Jesus came in the flesh to be the perfect sacrifice for us, to give us victory over Satan and grant us eternal love after our physical death. He was both fully man and fully God, our Shepherd, Teacher, Prophet, the Son of Man, and the Son of God. Jesus represented the Lamb without blemish, the perfect offering. Throughout His ministry, He served humanity, prayed for people, performed miracles, and ultimately died for us. Every drop of His blood is of immeasurable value in covering our sins and the sins of the world.

Dear reader, victory over Satan, as Revelation 12:11 states, comes through the blood of the Lamb and the word of our testimony. May the blood of Jesus work powerfully in your life as you proclaim the Word of God, place your faith in Christ, and testify to His goodness. Together, these elements make us victorious over the schemes of Satan. It is my prayer that this book blesses every reader and that the Lord will reveal Himself to you in the same way He has shown Himself to me.

Jesus is our intercessor, praying for us continually. As we see in Luke 23, He prayed for those who persecuted Him, and after ascending to heaven, He continues to intercede for us before the Father. He is our advocate (1 John 2:1-2). God loves us and desires a daily relationship and communion with us. I would like to close this book with a verse from Ecclesiastes.

Ecclesiastes 3:11 says, "He has made everything beautiful in its time. He has also set eternity in the human heart; yet no one can fathom what God has done from beginning to end."

In this verse, I believe that God is reminding us of His eternal plan for redemption. Our lives are part of the redemption story of fallen humanity, and through the blood of Jesus Christ, we have been restored. However, our human nature often prevents us from fully understanding why God does what He does or why He does it when

He does it. Yet, we can trust that everything happens in God's perfect timing and according to His plan.

God has set eternity in the human heart. Unlike animals, we are aware that our lives are not finite – we have a deep sense of eternity. We know that after our physical death, there is more beyond this world. While we may not always understand how or why God works in the ways He does, we can rely on the truth that His plan is good, and we can trust that all things work together for our good and His glory (Romans 8:28).

We believe that God's plan for us is eternal – that we will live with Him forever – but how this will unfold remains beyond our comprehension. Our task is to rest in peace and faith, knowing that God's plan for each of us, His sons and daughters, is good. We can trust that He is in control and that everything will work according to His will. Colossians 3:11 reminds us that "God has created all in all." John 1:3 reinforces this idea, saying, "Through Him all things were made; without Him nothing was made that has been made."

God is the Creator of everything, and His hands are at work in all that happens. We can have confidence and trust in Him, knowing that He is sovereign over all things.

Jesus Christ invites us to remain in a constant relationship with Him. He has already paid the price for us with His precious blood. This sacrifice, made on the cross, offers us grace and mercy, allowing us to enter into His holy presence through prayer, meditation, and reading the Bible. Despite living in a fallen, broken, and often chaotic world, we can be in consistent communion with Him, experiencing peace and joy because He is with us until the end of time.

Finally, we have the assurance that we will see Him again and live with Him forever in the new earth and new heaven (Revelation 21:1-4).

Glory to God in the highest, and to His Son, Jesus Christ, who was crucified for us and shed His blood so that we might have eternal life with Him in heaven.

www.ingramcontent.com/pod-product-compliance
Lightning Source LLC
Chambersburg PA
CBHW050727010526
44107CB00009B/761